RISE, THE FOUR ELEMENTALS

RISE, THE FOUR ELEMENTALS

Lead Yourself to a Life of Courage, Truth, Creativity, and Love by Awakening the Wisdom Within

BY NICK SENECA JANKEL

Rise, The Four Elementals: Lead Yourself to a Life of Courage, Truth, Creativity, and Love by Awakening the Wisdom Within

Library of Congress Cataloging-in-Publication Data
Library of Congress Control Number: 2022949605
Jankel, Nick Seneca 1974–

First Edition, January 2023
California, United States
Switch On Books
130pp.
Philosophy. Leadership. Self-Help. Graphic Novels and Comic Books.

Printed in the United States and United Kingdom—and wherever books are sold.

Illustrations by Tom Gravestock.

ISBN 978-1-9997315-8-8 (print book)
ISBN 978-1-9997315-9-5 (ebook)

Switch On Books London & Los Angeles

www.switchonnow.com

Discounts are available on quantity purchases by corporations, associations, and others.

For details, contact the publisher through the website above.

This book is designed to support, educate, inform, and inspire, but it is not meant or intended to diagnose, treat, cure, or prevent any disease. Medical advice should be obtained from a physician or qualified health practitioner to work with any mental or physical health issues. There are no guarantees expressed or implied.

OTHER BOOKS BY NICK SENECA JANKEL

Switch On: Unleash Your Creativity And Thrive With
The New Science And Spirit Of Breakthrough

The Book of Breakthrough: How to Use Disruptive Innovation
To Create A More Thriving World For All

Become A Transformational Organization: Galvanize Agility
Without Losing Stability To Survive And Thrive In The Digital,
Disrupted, And Damaged World

Spiritual Atheist: A Quest to Unite Science and Wisdom Into
a Radical New Life Philosophy to Thrive in the Digital Age

Now Lead the Change: Repurpose Your Career, Future-Proof
Your Organization, and Regenerate Our Crisis-Hit World
by Mastering Transformational Leadership

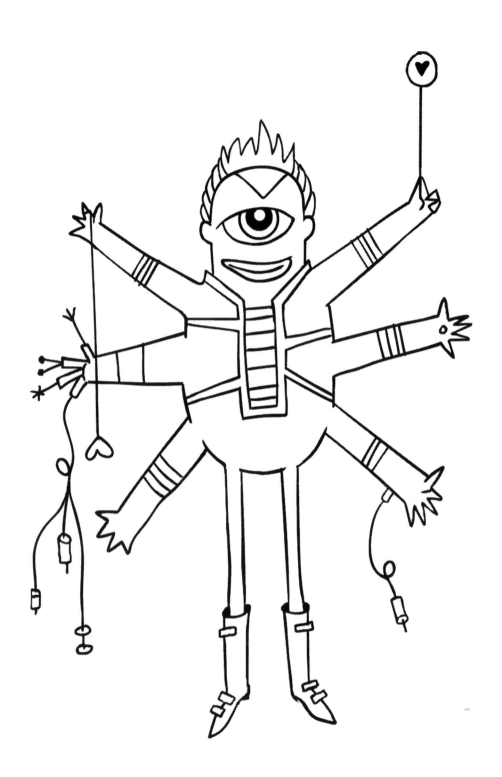

ABOUT NICK SENECA JANKEL

With over 20 years of hard-won experience advising leaders on the front lines of disruption, Nick Jankel is one of the world's preeminent practitioners of, and keynote speakers on, transformational and wise leadership. He has worked with over 100,000 leaders in organizations like Google, Pfizer, Nike, PlayStation, Microsoft, and LEGO. He has a Triple First from Cambridge University in Medical Science and Philosophy of Science.

Nick is the lead architect of Bio-Transformation®, a breakthrough method to drive change as fast as humanly possible in people, teams, and companies. It is underpinned by the latest brain, behavioral, and complexity science united with trauma-informed psychology and wisdom and practices from the contemplative sciences. With Bio-Transformation®, and the coherent Self-to-System™ leadership curriculum it powers, Nick advises entrepreneurs and C-Suite executives of ambitious organizations on how to transform themselves, their enterprises, and the systems from the inside out.

Nick is a co-founder of leadership consultancy Switch On Worldwide and cutting-edge sustainability agency FutureMakers. He has taught at Yale, London Business School, and Oxford and has coached celebrities and addicts on two international TV shows (BBC and MTV). Nick is the father of two, enjoys walking his dog in the woods, and loves nothing more than dancing to, and occasionally DJing (badly), disco, funk, hip hop, and house music. He is a dedicated student of the wisdom traditions.

www.switchonnow.com
www.futuremakers.global

Written for my son Jai.

I am here for you, in any way, in every way,
at all times, no matter what.
I see you. I trust you. I believe in you. I learn from you.

Darling, I know that in the past several years,
you have suffered a lot. I'm sorry. I don't want that.
I want your happiness, your safety, your freedom,
and your joy.
—Thích Nhất Hạnh, Buddhist Monk &
Founder of Plum Village

Wisdom alone is the science of other sciences.

—Plato

All that we are is the result of what we have thought.
The mind is everything.
What we think, we become.

—Buddha

When I despair, I remember that all through history, the way of
truth and love has always won . . . think of it always.

—Mahatma Gandhi

CONTENTS

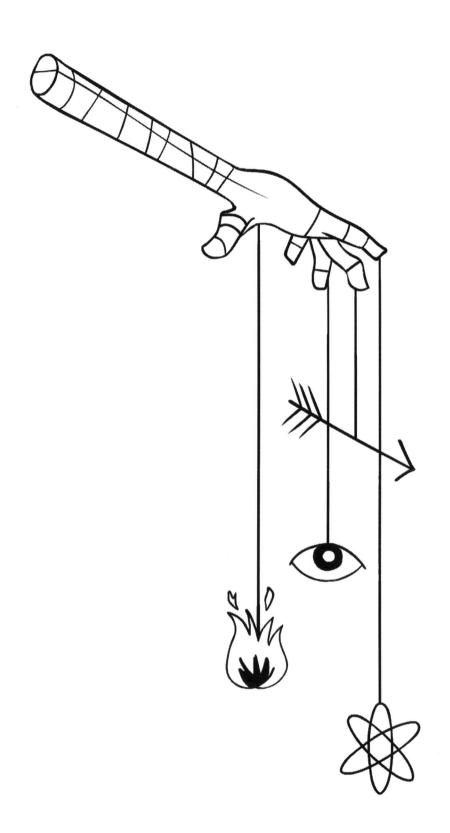

INTRODUCTION

If you want to get straight into the action—awakening the wisdom within yourself in the form of the everyday leadership superpowers of courage, truth, creativity, and love—then turn over a few pages and begin with Part 1. If you want to understand why I wrote this book, how it is designed to work for you, and where the philosophies, ideas, science, and wisdom shared within it come from, then this introduction is your starting point.

The origins of this book began when the older of my two sons went through some challenging times as he entered adolescence. Wanting to support him by providing him with some of the tools and methods that I have learned are essential for dealing with the more difficult moments in life, I gave him a copy of my first book. It sets out a breakthrough method for self-help that anyone can use to cope with the problems they experience in life—no matter how gnarly those problems are. The book describes a 10-step pathway we can use to flourish not despite life's problems, *but because of them.*

My son is a very bright young man. However, he found the book hard to get into, and, being frank with his father, he said it was "a little boring." Ouch. On reflection, I realized it was hardly surprising he didn't get into it, given it wasn't written for a young adult starting out on the adventure of life. So I made a mental note to think about ways I could share with him what I've learned about how to build a healthy, meaningful, exciting, yet peaceful life. I also mused that a book that shared my approach to life's challenges in an unorthodox way—simple, playful, engaging—might be of value to many who don't like reading conventional non-fiction books.

After a few more months of watching him struggle with ever-more intense challenges, I began to think seriously about how I could engage him in some of the life-changing wisdom, tools, and hacks I have gleaned from my fifty-odd years on this planet. After all, teaching these ways of living, loving, and leading is how I serve the world and how I earn a livelihood for my family. The design challenge I set myself with this book was this: how can I share, in a compelling way, how we can all become personal leaders in our lives? I mean leaders who take charge of their challenges; find effective ways to break through obstacles; and bring more harmony, courage, compassion, and inventiveness into difficult moments and everyday relationships.

When my son was about to turn thirteen, which in my cultural heritage marks a milestone and rite of passage, I put pen to paper. The result of this creative journey is contained in this book. What follows is a richly-illustrated and rhyming poem about the wisdom we all need to survive in our challenging times; and how we might be able to thrive not despite the adversity and anxiety we all face but even because of it. It has been written by me, a caring father and leader of leaders, to offer you bite-size pieces of wisdom for how to lead yourself to a life full of meaning, belonging, well-being, inner peace, and happiness in our age of multiple crises and both intense personal and shared challenges.

. . .

At the core of life are 'problems.' This is normal. Nature solves novel problems through the creativity shown by living organisms as they adapt to new pressures from their environment. The result of this adaptability, which is at the core of life itself, is the marvel of evolution. Over millions of years, the capacity to solve new problems creatively has led to astonishing species that can thrive in pretty much every environment on this incredible Earth. The complex life we see on our planet is premised on breaking through problems with creativity, courage, cleverness, and—for human beings at least—compassion.

Human beings are the only organism we are aware of that can solve problems with care and creativity through *conscious choice*. We are the only organism we know of that can choose to be courageous and strong even when we feel full of fear and trepidation. We seem to be the only organism that can reach out with love and empathy even when others are hating and raging. We seem to be the only organism that can seek truth and justice when those around us manipulate, deceive, and bully.

In fact, you are reading this today because your ancestors rose to overcome their challenges with resilience, intelligence, inventiveness, empathy, wisdom . . . and sheer style! You are reading this because your forebears made it. You are already a winner, even if you don't always feel like it.

The more challenges we face, the more our safety and happiness are threatened, for sure . . . but, also, the more opportunities we have to rise to the challenges, find hidden superpowers within us to break through them, and, in doing so, unlock our full potential. Problems, when approached wisely, bring out the very best in us.

This insight is at the core of every great story. In most stories, everyday folk—who are talented but not yet fully developed as leaders—encounter big problems in the form of terrifying monsters, deadly dragons, and brutal baddies. If they find ways to tap into their hidden skills and develop new superpowers, they can defeat their enemies—from Darth Vader to Lord Voldemort—and so become true heroes or heroines.

We are all in our own adventure story. We all start out talented but underdeveloped. It is up to us what happens next. We get to choose whether we seek to *avoid* our problems, perhaps by disappearing into iPhone screens or going along with the crowd; *fight* our problems, by becoming angry, dismissive, or rebellious (this is called "acting out"); or *transform* our problems by resolving them, and dissolving then, with as many superpowers as we can muster. These are the only options any human being has to choose from. We can retreat from, repress, ignore, fight, hate, or try to 'crush' our problems; or we can find ways to solve them with extraordinary superpowers that we can all build within us (to some degree and in some way).

Life is no more or less challenging today than it was for our hunter-gatherer ancestors. It is just that the nature of the problems has changed. Early humans had to rise to the challenges of snakes in the dark, saber-tooth tigers hunting them down, Ice Ages, tribal warfare, Vikings pillaging and killing, death at thirty, no toothpaste, and much else. Their bold and creative responses to such adversities have resulted in what we now call "civilization."

We invented technologies to keep out the predators and light up the dark nights. We invented ways to keep food flowing to large cities, planes to take us around the world, and human rights that, in many places but sadly not all, provide each citizen with safety from oppression. We are now being threatened by different problems. We must rise to social challenges, like climate change, civic unrest, post-truth politics, interminable culture wars (woke vs. alt-right), and vast economic inequality. We must rise to personal challenges, like anxiety, depression, divorce, technology and substance addictions, school violence, and online bullying.

Such problems are at the core of all human lives. This is the nature of things. But suffering, being in constant pain and fear, experiencing loneliness and anxiety, feeling cynical and frustrated because of our problems . . . these are anything but inevitable. There is another way, the path of wisdom. The more we build wisdom within, the easier it becomes to vanquish our inner "demons" (like self-doubt, anxiety, and loneliness) and our outer "enemies" too (like bullies, exams, first dates, and college interviews).

. . .

But there is a big but. Our advanced civilization, with its complex education system, teaches us remarkably little about how to identify, develop, and master personal leadership qualities like courage, truth, love, and creativity. These are the core superpowers that the "Four Elementals"—imaginative superhero characters within us that we can decide to wake up—can unlock. More on them in a moment.

While schools and universities have become brilliant at imparting knowledge to us about how our world works, they often miss out on sharing the tools and methods we need to navigate through our complex, uncertain, and scary world without collapsing into depression, apathy, and anxiety; or trying to cope by becoming addicted to success, substances, and screens.

I went to a top London private school and then two of the top ten universities in the world. Yet throughout my period of study, nobody gave me a single lesson on how to develop the superpowers of love, truth, courage, and creativity so I could thrive in my life. It is little wonder that I spent more than two decades dealing with chronic depression, fibromyalgia (chronic pain syndrome), work and food addictions, agonizing loneliness, and crippling social anxiety. I really struggled.

On top of blind posts in our education systems, we have forgotten the rites of passage that once initiated everyday heroines and heroes to lead their tribes by awakening their wisdom within. Few of us have access to the ways of old that invited young adults to wake up from the dreams of childhood and become leaders that walk the talk of love, truth, creativity, and courage. We have precious few rituals and practices, that are passed down to us from our elders, to help us to embrace and embody such superpowers.

This makes our lives unnecessarily difficult, painful, stressful, and full of anxiety. Our problems can then mount up and become fully-fledged mental health crises. Unresolved problems also get passed between generations. Most of us inherit inner emotional pain (called "intergenerational trauma"), negative beliefs, and self-sabotaging habits from our parents, grandparents, and possibly long-dead ancestors. We then have to deal with these *on top of all the problems* of our own life and era.

In my close family, we have faced degenerative diseases, neglect, abuse, bullying, substance addiction, suicide, body image issues, anxiety, obesity, obsessive-compulsive disorder, divorce, depression, dyslexia, missing siblings, abandonment, early death of a parent, and, like everyone, loss of cherished loved ones. Going back just two generations, we have had to cope with the trauma of war, genocide and the Holocaust, racism, poverty, life-threatening infectious diseases, persecution, and forced migration—whose echoes each person in our family must still deal with today on top of their own personal problems.

Every family has its own list of inherited pain, negative beliefs, self-sabotaging habits, and difficult problems that it has to cope with, including some of the anxieties and adversities unique to our own age: Covid lockdowns, grinding inequality, the constant worry of climate change, the renewed threat of nuclear war, toxins and pollution everywhere damaging our health, and weaponized digital algorithms sucking our attention to make money for a few. I am sure you can write a long list like this. This is something we all share, and we can take comfort in knowing that we really are all in this together.

Without the rites of passage that have long-helped young people become strong and wise members of the community—and with so little wisdom being taught in our schools and universities—it is little wonder that most teenagers will struggle. This is one reason why the number of young adults dealing with profound mental health problems has skyrocketed in our age of climate collapse, pandemics, economic inequality, and addictive digital technologies. Anxiety is one of the fastest-growing illnesses in developed countries. Suicide kills more young people than ever. Depression and despair haunt millions.

I have witnessed countless young adults, in the communities I am part of, struggling with addiction, suicidal ideation, OCD, loneliness, extremism, bullying, abuse, neglect, exclusion, and so much more. We are living through a period in which our younger people are finding it harder and harder to cope with a world that is ever more dangerous, depressing, and distracting (though also full of hope, possibility, and innovation). Empowering young adults to be able to rise to these challenges—and resolve and dissolve them creatively and courageously—has never been more critical or urgent.

■ ■ ■

When I was a troubled teen, I was put into psychotherapy for three years (aged thirteen to sixteen). It helped. I returned to it again during university and in my twenties. I still see a couple of therapists, from time to time, to help me process the rich challenges of being an entrepreneur, parent, and life partner. But valuable as therapy is, and was back then, it didn't quite reach the deepest parts of my pain or unlock the furthest reaches of my potential.

So when, at the age of 29, I had another meltdown—my start-up company, my intimate relationship, and my mental and physical health all tanked—I decided I needed to do whatever it took never to be that messed up again. There and then, I decided to leave no stone unturned until I could find a way to feel *consistently* peaceful, empowered, loving and loved.

Thankfully, help was at hand—lots of it—once I knew where to search.

Given that I had studied the best science and medicine the developed world has to offer—and tried solutions like psychotherapy and coaching—I knew I must be missing something. Casting aside my skeptical scientist's resistance to all things I considered weird, woo-woo, and woolly, I read every philosophical text and took every transformational workshop I could find. On this deep dive, I discovered that, for many millennia, philosophers, leaders, and culture keepers have been collecting and collating the insights that their cultures had discovered to 'win' at life.

Over tens of thousands of years, wise individuals have learned ways to deal with life's inherent problems and the pain and suffering they usually cause. They shared their tips, insights, and tools with their descendants through stories, songs, and performances. Once written languages evolved, cultures could codify, keep safe, and transmit the wisdom of their best teachers, thinkers, guides, and rulers forever. Collectively known as the "wisdom traditions," this great storehouse of insights and practices for thriving in life is invaluable.

When I was at school, I had no clue that such wisdom existed—let alone that there are libraries full of books containing hints, rules, and secrets for flourishing. All I was taught was *knowledge*: facts about biology, geography, history, and the like. Knowledge is fascinating and useful but it doesn't tell us that much about how to find happiness, good friendships, or a meaningful career. For this, we need wisdom.

Wisdom is not factual, although it is always grounded in the real and the tangible. Wisdom is not scientific, although cutting-edge scientific studies increasingly support it. Wisdom is, instead, a collection of insights—and practices we can use each day—that have proven valuable for many people to bring more peace, honor, compassion, empathy, meaning, belonging, health, wholeness, and happiness into the midst of the heartbreaking moments and most challenging situations.

Wisdom may not enable us to *solve* every problem. Some problems, like the loss of a loved one or the loss of biodiversity that has occurred in our rainforests, cannot be solved. Such genies cannot be stuffed back into the bottle. But we can always *dissolve* the pain and the stress that a problem causes us by expanding our consciousness. This means that we can harness any problem we face to become more loving, courageous, truthful, and creative as people. Wisdom ensures we can either solve, resolve, or dissolve our problems.

In the wisdom traditions, there is wisdom about how to: heal our worried minds and hurt hearts so we can always feel that we are enough, even when we are judged and criticized; find our truth in a world where lies are more and more the norm; love ourselves fully, forgive ourselves completely, and believe in ourselves totally (while always being humble and open to new experiences); discover what vocational subjects and practical activities give us most meaning and fulfillment; approach dating, love, and sex with honesty, integrity, kindness, and playfulness; build authentic and caring relationships through humility, commitment, and compassion.

This last challenge, to have deeply rewarding relationships based on unconditional love—with strong boundaries but no strings attached—is perhaps the hardest challenge that life asks us to rise to. To develop a few strong and *reciprocal* relationships with parents, friends, and, eventually, life partners and children—where we get back as much as we give, and we are loved as much as we love—is probably the most important way to guard against mental health challenges. The world's longest research study on human development, the Harvard Study, tells us that nourishing relationships is the single most important factor for a lifetime of happiness.

Wisdom supports us in building nourishing relationships even when many around us seem defensive, selfish, or withdrawn. It helps us to feel whole in a family, society, or world that often feels fragmented. It empowers us to stay hopeful when all we read in the news seems depressing. It encourages us to realize that some of what we watch on TikTok, Netflix, or Youtube may be a distraction from our more difficult feelings. It allows us to approach our most scary and upsetting challenges with a sense of power, hope, and optimism.

Wisdom can make the difference between crumbling under the intensity of exams, peer pressure, family expectations, dating, bullying, and so much more . . . and rising to these life challenges with an abundant sense of courage, truth, love, and creativity.

This wisdom of the world belongs to us all. It is our collective birthright. We should all have access to the vast treasure trove of insights on, and practices for, dealing with challenges, coping with crises and living in harmony with one another. Whether wisdom contained in Taoism from China, Zen Buddhism from Japan, yoga and Hindu philosophy from India, Sufi poems from Persia and Turkey, Norse myths from Scandinavia, the shamanic practices of the Amazon or Siberia, the philosophies of Ancient

Greece and Rome, or the writings of the mystics of medieval Europe, there is so much for us to learn that can help us to lead a thriving life.

. . .

I firmly believe, having worked with over 100,000 senior executives in major firms like Nike and Microsoft to develop wiser and more creative leadership—as well as coached and taught tens of thousands of individuals across all walks of life—that we each have within us the wisdom we need to rise up to *all* of the challenges life presents us with. However, the awakening of our greatest superpowers rarely happens by accident. It takes just as much time and commitment as getting to a great university or becoming a great sportsperson.

While we all have wisdom inherent in our bodies—our bodies can heal a cut or bruise without our knowledge—we often need help from antiseptic creams, antibiotics, chemotherapy, vaccinations, and surgeons. Our minds also can heal emotional and mental pain too. However, they also need some help. Help comes in the form of professional support like psychotherapy, CBT, counseling, coaching, and complementary therapies. However, there are many things we can do to empower *ourselves* to find more wholeness and happiness. There are very obvious things like doing exercise, getting good sleep, and exploring probiotics. Then there is cultivating wisdom.

Wisdom comes in the form of *insights* that unlock our imagination, intelligence, courage, and compassion; and *practices* that actually change the state of our nervous systems so we become more strong, harmonic, creative, and loving. Wisdom practices range from meditation to martial arts. You'll discover, later on, a color code I have put together to help you categorize wisdom practices and understand what they may be doing inside us. Through a combination of learning and doing, we can all awaken the wisdom within us to find much more well-being, healing, meaning, and belonging in our lives, *no matter how challenging things get.*

In fact, the wisdom and practices in this book are designed to provide a foundation of resilience that can help to "immunize" you against future mental health challenges. The more we develop durable and powerful feelings of love, courage, truth, and creativity inside—by cultivating wisdom within—the more likely it is that we can prevent our problems, which are inevitable, from mushrooming into full-blown psychological or emotional disorders, which are not. Awakening our own wisdom, therefore, is a preventative measure we can all take to lessen the chances that stressful events will send us into the kind of psychological meltdowns, breakdowns, and burnouts that I experienced so many times before I decided to wise up.

Now that I have been awakening the wisdom in me for almost twenty years—complemented by professional therapy and coaching when needed (as well as the basics like sleep hygiene, healthy eating, exercise, and tending to my microbiome)—I simply cannot imagine living a full, fulfilled, meaningful, and grounded life without taking refuge in wisdom insights and practices *each and every day*. Life today is just too darn challenging to endure without the resilience, inner peace, big-picture perspective, and sense of interconnection that wisdom unlocks.

■   ■   ■

In *Rise, The Four Elementals*, I have synthesized and summarized the wisdom I wish I had known as a troubled teenager; a life-loving but often depressed young adult; and a young leader in the start-up I co-founded when I was just 24. Within are some of the ideas, realizations, and wisdom I have had to learn the (very) hard way—through failure, nervous breakdown, and chronic mental and physical health challenges—that I would have loved to have been offered in my formative years by a mentor, ally, teacher, or author.

That said, please understand something crucial. This book is absolutely *not* meant to replace professional advice, clinical support, or psychotherapy. When we suffer from persistent mental health challenges it is *always* appropriate to seek professional clinicians who have the training and tools to help. In fact, seeking such support demonstrates advancing maturity and growing wisdom. Getting help is what all the most courageous and wise leaders do when they feel stuck.

On my deep dive, and even with a degree in philosophy, I found that much of the wisdom available is not that accessible or enjoyable to read. It often lives in dusty books, long diatribes, complex language, and arcane traditions. Many contemporary approaches to wisdom come within what I call "New Age packaging," which has never inspired or attracted me. For many years, I actively rejected books, methods, or movies with yin-yang symbols or whale music. While I have grown more tolerant, I still don't believe great wisdom requires a certain kind of branding.

After I had spent a good few years integrating wisdom into my everyday life so I could walk some of this talk, it became more and more clear that my purpose in life is to help others awaken the wisdom within so they can thrive in life, love, and especially leadership. One way to deliver on my purpose is to find innovative ways to bring profound, practical, and playful wisdom to as broad an audience as possible. This way, I can play some small part in co-creating a world that is wiser-led. This book is part of that mission.

As a former scientist, what I share within is grounded in the concrete realities of life and is free from doctrine and dogma of any kind. The wisdom in this book has nothing to do with God, gods, or ghosts. Although some ideas I will share with you come from traditions that do have such beings, I won't be talking about them. I make zero unsubstantiated claims about supernatural entities like spirit guides and offer no vague platitudes that provide little help with the deepest pain, and most significant problems, in life. Neither do I suggest that any religion, heritage, fashion, incense stick, or widget will solve our problems. Religious and cultural choices are deeply personal and not something that I ever comment on. What is in this book is wisdom that is universal. We can all awaken the wisdom within us, no matter our creed or ethnicity.

What has been exciting for me, as I've spent twenty years studying, reading, and practicing this wisdom for life, love, and leadership, is that cutting-edge 'hard' science increasingly backs up much of the timeless 'soft' wisdom that has been transmitted from generation to generation in the form of stories, poems, and philosophical treatises. Each week, thousands of academic papers are published on neuroscience, animal behavior, and experimental psychology. Some appear to confirm much of what the great wisdom teachers and wise leaders have been saying for millennia.

My greatest labor of love has been pulling together what we can glean from the wisdom traditions about having a good and meaningful life—and becoming a wise leader—with what we are learning about how our minds and bodies work from the latest science. I have turned this project into a pretty awesome curriculum for leaders—complete with tools, practices, and experiences— designed to empower anyone to confidently and consciously lead their people, and their organizations, toward a thriving future. It always starts with ourselves, though. Wisdom tells us that we can only truly transform the world if we do it *from the inside out*. We have to be the change we want to see in others, as Gandhi so famously implored.

As I could not find a rigorous theory upon which this curriculum could sit—one that unified science and wisdom in a coherent way—I built my own. I did this with the input of many great thinkers and my business partner, wife, and mother of my youngest son, Alison McAulay. The resulting effort is Bio-Transformation˙. Bio-Transformation˙ is an original method for unlocking lasting change in people, businesses, and systems as fast as humanly possible. Thirty years in the making, Bio-Transformation˙ is powered by the latest brain, behavioral, and complexity science, united with trauma-informed psychology and blended with insights and practices from the wisdom traditions, sometimes called the "contemplative sciences."

. . .

One place where the latest science and psychology—and ancient wisdom from myths and traditions—converge is in the different strategies we all have access to in order to solve difficult problems. We can solve difficulties with inner strength, breaking through blockages with courage. We can use creativity and imagination to invent new ways to do things that resolve our problems. We can harness reason to make sense of things and truth to blast through lies and deceit. And we can use love and compassion to dissolve our problems by bringing ourselves, and others, into connection, trust, and peace. Often we will need a blend of all four to really transform a problem for good.

Each of these four qualities can be seen as a superpower that we can *all* develop. Each strategy can be seen as the A-Game of one of four superheroes we all have dormant within us. Alison and I call them the Four Elementals. I invite you to imagine that you have these Four Elementals inside you right now: the Champion (superpowers of strength, grit, and courage), the Commander (superpowers of truth, harmony, and order), the Creator (superpowers of creativity, aliveness, and imagination), and the Connector (superpowers of love, kindness, and compassion). We can draw on these Elementals for fresh thinking, empowering emotions, and bold moves when faced with the hardest challenges.

While we all tend to develop the strengths of one or two of the Elementals as we grow up in our specific family setting, culture, and education system—some of us become more creative and inventive, some more intellectual and ordered, some more kind and caring, some more strong and action-oriented—it is vital to know that the superpowers of all four of the Elementals are available to everyone on this planet *at any time they call upon them*.

We developed the Four Elementals by standing on the shoulders of giants. One of them is the great psychologist Carl G. Jung, who popularized the concept of "archetypes" a hundred or so years ago. This idea has been instrumental in inspiring our work on the Four Elementals. More shoulders we have stood on are the psychoanalysts and mythologists James Hillman, Robert Moore, Joseph Campbell, and Jean Bolen. These stellar thinkers and practitioners have used ancient myths and profound psychology to deepen Jung's work on archetypes.

The Four Elementals you are about to meet are not just rooted in myth, psychology, and the wisdom traditions. In the last decade or so, cutting-edge neuroscience has provided compelling evidence that we all have (at least) four signature neural networks across our brains and bodies—complete with cocktails of specific neurotransmitters and hormones that flow when they are activated—that have evolved over millions of years to give us brilliant ways to deal with the various problems of life.

We have a brain network optimized for control and prediction (truth, order, and intellect) and one optimized for creativity (imagination and invention). We have a whole-body network optimized for protection and safety (courage and strength) and one optimized for relaxation and connection (love, compassion, and empathy). Science is also providing us with more and more knowledge about how intense childhood experiences, adversity, difficult memories, and overwhelming emotions actually change how these networks, and neurotransmitters, function.

Putting all this together, we get the Four Elementals. Each Elemental offers us a unique and powerful way of solving life's problems. The Cambridge University Dictionary defines 'elemental' with two sentences, both relevant to us and this book. The first is "showing the strong power of nature: elemental force/fury." This speaks to the primordial, utterly natural forces within us that we can use to solve problems, harassing one of the four superpowers: courage, truth, creativity, and love. The second definition is "basic or most simple, but strong." These four superpowers are the most basic yet dynamic and potent ways we have to engage with life's problems—challenges in school, work, relationships, intimacy, culture, politics, and climate change—and rise to each with our full potential.

■ ■ ■

I have always loved the stories of heroic characters—like those in Marvel movies or graphic novels like *V for Vendetta*—who discover superpowers inside that they can use to save the world (and themselves in the process). Heroic characters exist in stories—a powerful form for transmitting wisdom from one person or generation to the next—to show us what is possible if we commit to our own personal development as much as we commit to achieving good exam results, having fun, or getting a decent job.

Many great novel and movie characters have found a way to make lemonade from the lemons that life has given them. They have found a way to transform their problems into awesome superpowers. The X-Men franchise is my favorite story that brings this essential wisdom to life. Each X-person has a genetic mutation that makes them different, weird, scary to others, and rejected. Each of them has to go on a journey to turn their greatest weaknesses into their greatest strengths.

The natural force and energy of the Four Elementals match perfectly with the idea of a superhero with unique superpowers. But, just as every superhero has weaknesses—kryptonite (*Superman*), rage (*Batman*), and even porcelain (*X-Men*'s Jean Grey)—each Elemental has weaknesses too. When we use an Elemental's superpower, their problem-solving strategy, *too much,* we become 'addicted.' Just like the Sith are addicted to the power of the Force in *Star Wars*, when we are addicted, we turn the Elemental into a bit of a fiend. I share in the book what to look out for so you can avoid making such tragic mistakes as much as possible.

On the other hand, just as Luke Skywalker initially denies his Jedi potential to focus on his "day job," we can also become 'allergic' to a superpower. This is when we don't know how to access an Elemental's problem-solving strategy or are afraid of its force. This makes us weak and powerless in that domain. This also allows one of the other Elementals to dominate us, which leads right back to addictions. The ideal is to be somewhere between 'allergic' and 'addicted' to each superpower—and in a balance between the Four Elementals.

To become wise like this is a lifetime's work of self-awareness, self-development, and maturity, so we must not expect too much from ourselves too early. I am certainly nowhere near "cooked" after twenty years of learning and practicing such wisdom. However, by regularly tapping into the Four Elementals over a sustained period, we can learn how to harmonize their superpowers, minimize addictions and allergies, and integrate them together into the form of an everyday leader.

The journey is the destination. The experience of becoming a heroic character in our own epic movie—defeating "evil" time and time again by constantly growing our superpowers—is *the* adventure of a lifetime.

■ ■ ■

The word 'character' is key. In our work helping efficient managers turn into wise, creative, and courageous leaders, we distinguish 'personality' from 'character'. We all have a personality, but it is not necessarily who we really are deep down. Our personality is usually made up of all the ways we have developed to cope with the stresses of life. We may have become 'cool', 'smart', 'funny', or 'quiet' to avoid dangers and threats. We then use and overuse these strategies to get our needs met as best we can . . . but we lose parts of our genuine character in the process.

For example, becoming 'cynical' can protect us from feeling let down by a parent or by life, but it may also rob us of our enthusiasm and potential to do great things. Being 'smart' may help us get through exams and get the praise of parents or teachers, but it can also stop us from being vulnerable, sensitive, and open to new things. Being 'funny' may get some people to like us, but it can also stop us from feeling connected, respected, and loved. I know this myself as I have tried all three of these coping mechanisms, and many more, in the past. They helped for a bit to protect me and keep me safe. But, eventually, they started to fail me and kept me locked in.

In other words, our personality is not who we are but *whom we have had to become* to deal with life. We all learn to morph ourselves to be liked, respected, seen, or just plain safe, but these ways of coping also block us from some of the things we want most, like well-being, meaning, and belonging. Leaders have to let go of their personalities in order to reveal their true characters within.

Our authentic character—the unique leader or superhero we all have waiting within—is revealed in the dark and difficult times when we choose to be loving and compassionate rather than angry or afraid. It is forged in the flames of adversity when we choose to stand firm in courage rather than be floored by fear. It is unleashed in times of deception, manipulation, and "fake news" when we tell the truth, even when it means risking the approval of those we care about.

Our true character is revealed when we stand against bullies, risking social rejection rather than taking the easy way out by running away or joining in. It is demonstrated when we ask for help from our parents, friends, or professionals rather than pretending everything is okay. It shines through when we stop saying that we "don't care" and once again put ourselves at risk of disappointment by having big dreams and noble aspirations.

The Four Elementals are here to help you to locate and embody your true character. This book is here to help you step up as the unique leader you are by expressing the superpowers of love/compassion, truth/harmony, strength/courage, and creativity/imagination in your own special way. This is a way to find your authentic character as a leader in life.

By leader, I don't just mean a senior manager or executive. I mean someone who shapes their own destiny with creativity, courage, and care. Leadership exists when we are not slaves to circumstances and we don't allow ourselves to become victims of the habits and beliefs of others.

Leadership exists when we move through fear and self-judgment to step confidently yet humbly toward our goals.

Leadership means not succumbing to cynicism and complacency but always keeping hope and imagination alive. Leadership means taking a stand on climate change and social injustice—that costs us in some way—while others are apathetic or afraid. Leadership exists when we love and care for ourselves properly, not as some trendy lifestyle choice but as a radical form of self-determination and service to others.

Being a leader means speaking the truth even when it is uncomfortable. It means apologizing freely when we hurt people, especially when it is the last thing we feel like doing! It means diving inside ourselves, as deep as may be necessary, to find our way out of stress, anxiety, and anger. It means not giving in to peer pressure or the culture wars but instead leading our friends to more healthy, whole, and happy places. Leadership means not letting our parents or our educators tell us who we should be but forging our own destinies (while respecting the needs of others and our planet).

. . .

With the Four Elementals as inspirations and guides, I have attempted to collect in this book some of the most elemental wisdom one might need to survive and flourish as a (young) adult in this beguiling and exciting world—powered by a fusion of timeless insights and timely scientific breakthroughs. This book's ultimate purpose is to provide a bedrock of wisdom upon which you can build a life of learning, growth, intimacy, joy, happiness, service, meaningful success, and wise leadership.

As I wrote down on paper the first words of the book, the text started to take shape. But rather than prose, which I am used to writing, a rhyming poem appeared on the pages. I wasn't sure whether to keep going with this form, as poetry is definitely not my A-Game, but as it seemed to flow out of me, I went with this creative experiment and the risks it entails! Choosing a fixed four-line rhyming pattern added a creative constraint that challenged me to write with as much clarity and brevity as possible. I hope my experiment works for you.

Thinking about what stories inspired me most when I was a young adult, I decided to bring the wisdom to life with illustrations. I have always adored graphic novels. I used to avidly read the legendary sci-fi comic *2000AD* each week as a kid; and spent many hours devouring awesome books like *Watchmen* as a teenager and young adult. I still read the freshest graphic novels that come out each year. So I spent months looking for a fitting illustrator to collaborate with me. Tom Gravestock, based in Canada, has been a wonderful accomplice: supporting, challenging, inspiring, and illustrating some very big ideas in brilliant ways.

- In Part 1, I set out the Four Elementals and how to understand them as forces of potency and potential lying within us all. We can wake each one up and, in doing so, awaken its wisdom with us.

- In Part 2, I propose each Elemental's unique superpowers, gifts, and strategies—as well as their addictions and allergies. There is a 'Book' dedicated to each Elemental. Each Book ends with some exercises and practices you can use to awaken the wisdom of that Elemental.

- Part 3, I show how we can all become leaders—whether we are leaders of ourselves, our family, friendship group, class, team, workplace, or society—by integrating the Four Elementals inside. I point out some ways you can use all Four Elementals together to lead yourself towards well-being, happiness, great friendships, a supportive community, intimate relationships, meaningful careers, and making a difference in our world.

- The book concludes with an Appendix listing some of the characteristics of the Four Elementals in one place.

This book is meant to be helpful to you right now and be a support for you in the future. The road is long, with many a winding path, and with much adversity. It is here to serve you in your journey to becoming happy, purposeful, peaceful and loved—as we all deserve to be. It is here to inspire and encourage you to keep going in the most challenging moments and also to enrich you and help you expand when you're feeling most up-for-life, energized, and bold.

Pick it up when you're feeling stuck or stressed. Find a stanza or sutra that gives you some support with what you are dealing with right now. But also pick it up when you feel ready for a new 'upgrade' and want to accelerate your personal development with fresh insights and stimulation.

According to my experience and that of most of my clients, there seem to be limitless numbers of wisdom, mindset, and leadership 'upgrades' available as we journey through the adventure of life. My hunch is that this is, in some way, the point. It's as if we are in an endless real-life role-playing game with infinite numbers of 'bosses' to beat (usually our fears and sabotaging habits, as opposed to baddies, however, people who do bad things really do exist). Before we reach each new boss level, there seems to be another power-up available to us—at just the right time—in the form of a wise and creative breakthrough. I find this rather awesome, mysterious, and exciting.

Buyer beware. Within this book is a sketch of *my* map for making sense of and forging a path through life's trials and tribulations. Yet wisdom tells us that everyone has to find *their own* map. Inside is just what I sense, feel, and think is essential wisdom for leaders, young and old. The student or seeker of truth must always test out wisdom before adopting it. So approach everything you read with skepticism but not cynicism. Try things out. Keep what works.

Disregard—or perhaps store away for a future moment—what doesn't seem wise, helpful, or accurate. I may also be wrong or incomplete. I have written this book to be accessible; however, that doesn't mean everything within it will be relevant to you right now; or make sense in terms of who you are today. Often we're not yet ready to hear certain pieces of wisdom: we need to live, make mistakes, and learn before we're available to receive the next upgrade.

So, my fellow wisdom seekers and leaders in life, be ready to be challenged, stretched, and puzzled as you try—like we *all must* if we want to thrive—to make sense of the mysteries of achieving a good, true, and beautiful life.

Nick Seneca Jankel
Near Brighton, United Kingdom, September 2022

PART 1

PROLOGUE

THE CALL TO ADVENTURE

From the day we are born (and perhaps even earlier)
We are thrown into life's struggles—a lifetime journeyer
For the first few years, our only job is to grow and play
And learn how to eat, poop, and on two legs stay

If we're lucky, our first years will be safe, stable, loving, and calm
Years full of fun, games, and parental caring balms
Yet disappointments will arise and hurt each of our hearts
We will all have trials, tribulations, troubles, and worse

As we reach adolescence, big things start to change
We get hair, an identity, and may see those we fancy as strange
Our brain is expanding at an incredible rate
As we start to explore what might be beyond the gate

As we become adults, struggles increase; felt more keenly
Our hearts can get heavy, and words will be felt meanly
The great adventure is calling; now's the time to step up to the plate
And become a wise one who masters their own fate

Each of us becomes the Hero of our tale in adolescence
We are cast out on the path to find our unique essence
So let us start by stating what is eternally true
What will guide us forward when we don't have a clue

When we struggle, toss, turn—are afraid, hurt, and confused
Whenever we feel neglected, addicted, or abused
Remember that within us all are sources of limitless originality and
    courage
Four life forces that are unshakable and unbreakable right up to our
    death

All of us have within us a zest for life's endless curiosities
Superpowers of courage, truth, love, and creating novelties
So, from the earliest age; when we feel downcast or blue
We can tap into this font; learning what is eternally true

RISE, THE FOUR ELEMENTALS

At all times, we remember this truism: we're all already winners
Because millions of creatures had to make it for us to be sitting here:
    grinners
We have been given the two greatest gifts in the known universe
Life, and consciousness of it; and we don't even have to rehearse

We can explore life's mysteries of wisdom with relish: they're legendary!
They let us always be happy, hopeful, and whole—and live a life less
    ordinary
We are now ready to get fully into this book
A treasure trove of wisdom with which I have learned to my life cook

WAKING UP THE WISDOM

The human tribe has lost its way—with few rites of passage left
Which has left many of us feeling way too weak, lost, lonely, and bereft
Yet the ancients left us wisdom: superpowers and insane surprises
With which to navigate the path—and deal with whatever arises

From the moment we leave home and are exposed to harm
We must rely on these strengths to weather each storm
Such a superpower takes courage, diligence, and discipline to master
The rest of this tale is there to get you there much faster

In our bloodlines flow love, truth, creativity, and steel
But they will be useless in battle unless we get real
And choose to develop superpowers as the primary mission
Before we nail the great adventures and build a better world with our
    vision

As we move through our own story, vital parts of us must meet
Each of us can claim our birthright: to be strong, smart, sensitive, and
    sweet
There are four legends within us all waiting to be known
Ready to download their superpowers once they are shown

Like a gamer, we can try each character's skin
And feel their lightning bolts of genius enliven us within
But we much watch out for their darkness and their unique dangers, too
Lest we become destructive and deranged in all that we do

Each upgrade they offer is a martial art to be learned
Every super-power we gain must be effortfully earned
Each upgrade requires payment: commitment and care
Every investment returns power, wisdom, and courage to dare

It is time to wake up the wisdom within our bodies and minds
Without it, we cannot complete the adventures we find
With wisdom awake, we can access all of our potential
Enlivening our awareness with all that's essential

Waking up the wisdom means way more than studying knowledge and
facts

It means finding our way to freedom, to inner peace, to being totally
relaxed

It means glimpsing hope whether others see despair and things beastly

Finding a reliable source of love with which we can become whole,
happy, and free

INTRODUCING THE FOUR ELEMENTALS

Let us meet the four characters in our questing RPG
That have wisdom and weapons and spells to help us be free
Each lies dormant until we choose it to fiercely invoke
Then we make it our own as we become more awake and woke

We're going to explore four essential archetypes: the Four Elementals
Which together can solve any problem in health and happiness; small
    or monumental
Each Elemental has a Book containing their superpowers (and some
    weaknesses)
Prime wisdom that unlocks meaning, belonging, peace, and uniqueness

Once we open each Book and grasp what is so special
About each Elemental that we can spark in our vessel
We can then invoke them, invite them, and speak to them inside
And bring them together into a leader that in our wholeness resides

Think of each archetype, the Elementals, as seed stores in consciousness
That we can tap into to achieve our hopes and dreams in concreteness
Each is a neural network that can our world and ourselves regenerate
An electric current of potency that we can cultivate and propagate

First up is the Champion, who looks after our safety with grit, resilience,
    and responsibility
Then comes the Commander, who deals in smarts, order, and honesty
Then there's the Creator, who brings forth ideas, enthusiasm, and
    enlivenment
Last comes the Connector, who inspires love, care, and enlightenment

Each of us develops strengths in one or two Elementals
To survive our early life, fit the vibe of our family, and fulfill our potential
But each of us can, at any time, access the superpowers of all four
To live, love, and lead with a limitless roar

Each Elemental cares for different elements of life
But left alone, without balance, will lead us to strife
Each has luminous qualities and dazzling intensity
But, without wisdom, leads to shadow, dark sides, and density

Each Elemental has weak spots: unique kryptonite
Which leaves us either lacking or hooked, both a blight
We develop brother allergies and addictions to our Elemental proponents
Which stops us from growing, flowing, and having gorgeous moments

The Champion, when upset, goes vicious and violent, or a hapless victim
The Creator turns despondent, entitled, or just daydreams
The Connector slips into being flaky, fawning, and hypersensitive
The Commander descends into control freakery—misleading and
    manipulative

The aim of the game is to be all four Elemental at once
Or rather, to be able to use each when it suits the occurrence
Wielding each one's superpowers across all our dimensions
While bringing calm to each Elemental's trigger-happy tensions

Those who crack this code get life's ultimate buffs
Which will ensure they can break through when going gets tough
"Easter eggs for all" was the cry of all the wisdom keepers
Whether expert, veteran, or noob—we can all be reward reapers

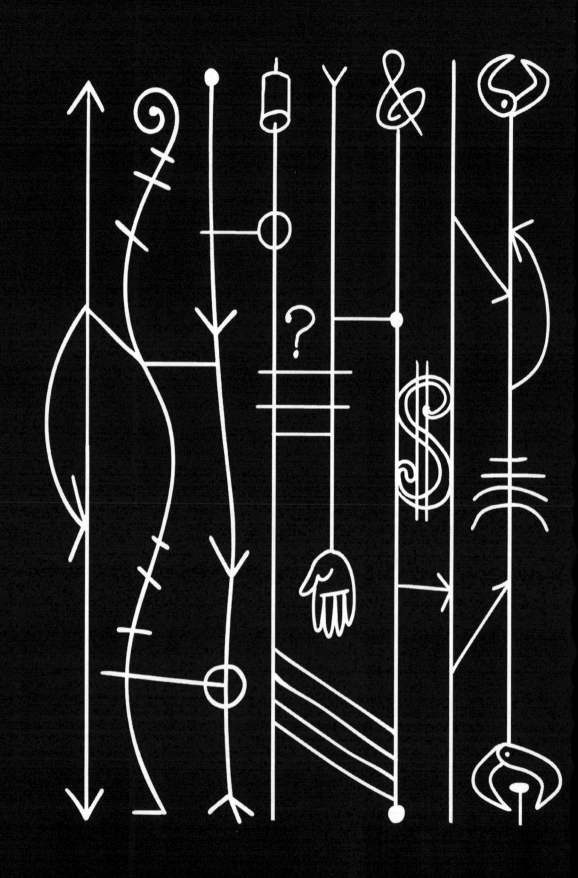

PART 2

THE BOOKS OF THE FOUR ELEMENTALS

FINDING UNSHAKEABLE COURAGE

Within us all—no matter who—is a force of magnificent strength
A super-hero that will goal-achieve, protect, and go to any length
To make things happen and to blast through all obstacles
The Champion protects the weak, is noble, and defeats all struggles

Armed with a live connection to the Champion, we can stop being a
    worrier
And instead, find the courage to step up as a bold Warrior
Strong, supple, and proud, the Warrior can be assertive
Without venting our rage or being reactive and aggressive

The Champ can power us to compete with all our might
Without becoming obsessed by crushing the rest outright
We can give our brain and brawn to finish first
While shining out a collaborative and playful sunburst

Tough times and disappointments will always occur
In every life, project, idea, exam, or love affair
The Champ makes sure we don't collapse in an inner implosion
When the going gets rough, we contain fiery emotions

The Champion achieves goals and gets chores done with grit
It can cope when the going gets tough and with inevitable boring bits
With it, we gain devotion, dependability, and fierce loyalty
We show up as constant, committed, and courageous: with true fidelity

The Champ can deliver all this and more
It will keep us stable and grounded from birth to death's door
Each Champion has the courage to deal with any battle
We can always dig deeper—and not get rattled

We must find a way to trust in the genius of this masculine nature
The mysteries of the sword ensure we become a self-creator
Then we can puncture, propel, pierce, protect, and provide
And turn rage into courage with compassion inside

At times, the perils that the Champ defends us from are really real
A few people, and situations, are a hazard; and can our fates seal
Some 2-5% of people can really hurt us—their hurt hearts are debased
But 95% plus of folk mean well and have their hearts in the right place

The Champ can—with force—break through any blockage
Have the courage to own our mistakes; be accountable for what we
    damage
It will do what it takes to protect us from dangers and trauma
And enable us to live with true-heartedness, not drama

A FORCE FOR GOOD

Stuff will happen, whether divorce, death, or disease
No Hero is not challenged to find their way back to the baby's natural
    ease
We all lose our innocence and become an orphan
The Champion will guard us; ensure we remain sovereign

When sucked into tech, success, or substance addiction
The Champion breaks free from such ruts and their fictions
When it feels like we must give up; we've got nothing left
Call on the Champion and its muscly heft

We can then give our all to whichever quest we are on
Dealing with sore muscles and exhaustion: and keep going on
We hold steadfast in our hearts that we're working for the greater good
But that doesn't mean we don't care for ourselves and our livelihood

The Champion at life drinks from their own powerful cup
Success is determined, in no small part, by simply never giving up
Our stumbling and humbling become our greatest strengths
As long as we connect to life's truest wavelengths

If we can sense when we feel empty or powerless
Or when our body and mind are flooded with intense angriness
With discipline, we can harness this oomph for goodness
And always ensure we stay open to relatedness

It is an art form to know when we should dig deep and push on
Or realize that a much-loved project or partnership is done
Always within are two guides—to decide on the mission
Cool, clinical reason—and warm, wondrous intuition

If the Champ feels unsure, uncomfortable, or afraid
We remember the words of all fathers to come to our aid
"You can do it, my love; just keep going!
You have within you way more than you are currently knowing."

"There is always more inside you," the Champ whispers when we're
   stuck
Although we may need time to process before we can level up
We are ready to sacrifice our comforts and ease
To deliver on the mission and not fight, flee or freeze

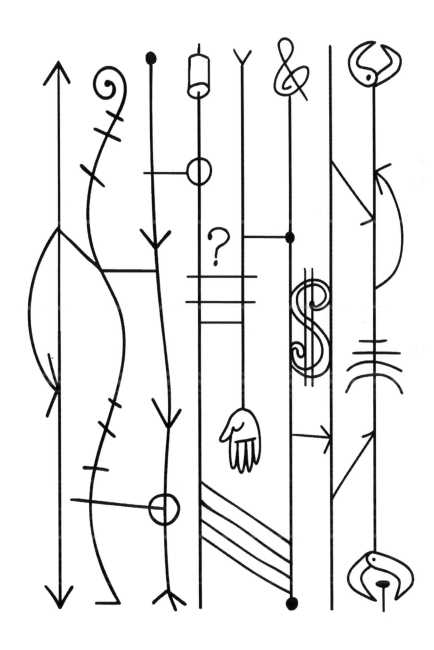

MAKING OUR OWN WAY

As we become adults, our path must become free
Of other's expectations—their manipulations—no matter their plea
We cannot be responsible for anyone else's lot
Their claims on our future must come to naught

The Champ ensures we break free of parental dependency
Without rejecting our people's help in our ascendency
It's more about moving from childhood fears and ignorance
Allowing us to break through limits; we are vigorous!

We marshal our power and get ready to brace
Then break free from social mores and find our own space
It is an art to fashion ourselves into what it's fitting for us to be
While remembering our family have a safe and loving place for we

Is it time to release some of our childish worries and charms
Without losing our childlike innocence, wonder, and calm
It is time to launch ourselves into the world—and independence claim
But there is no need to reject support, tenderness, and the fun of family
    board games

The Champion ensures we break free of all co-dependent chains
We choose our own path; without people-pleasing games
We need not heed glossy ads, YouTubers, or folks
All limit our potential to grow into vibrant oaks

We must always be sure that we cannot save our folks
With their issues and angsts, they alone must cope
Yet we can forgive them for all their wrongdoings
If we want to love others freely and live with stable moorings

The Champion burns bright; an archetypal Warrior
Takes on those that denigrate—and breaks through perceived barriers
We, therefore, choose wisely: only those with honor we befriend
Stand up for our morals—and the weak defend

The key to the Champ's power is to completely own
Our bullshit, mistakes, and errors that made us over-blown
Only once we take ownership of our 'stuff' can we break the barriers
That block us from achieving our bold goals as wizardly warriors

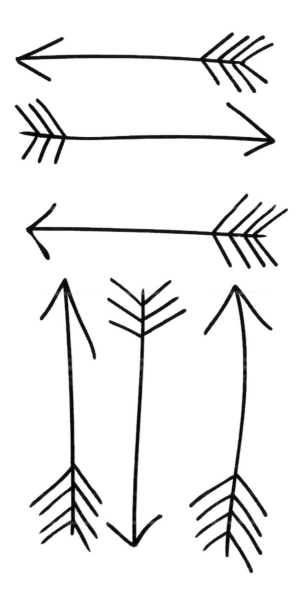

THE CHAMPION'S WEAK SPOTS

The Champion empowers us to be bold, confident, productive, and
brave
Cutting through blockages with resilience till the end of our days
But when we're addicted to the fight, we can be cut-throat and
obsessed
With winning, adrenaline—and from others' success, we theft

Champ can be so focused on busyness, energy, and adventure
That we forget how to be present, loving, and tender
It's easy to feel like the Champion is invincible
But our body and mind are precious—damage is predictable

In times of stress and social worries, some of us go a bit haywire
A crooked Champion can be cruel or 'cool': stuck in a mire
When our audacious energy fills our body with power
We may be tempted to take risks like drunk driving—or drugs devour

We must guard against abdicating our joyous tenderness
To win a victory and, because of it, lose togetherness
We must watch out for when we feel most powerless
And not take this pain out on others in poisonous cowardice

On the other hand, if our Champion is weak, passive, and low
We can be sheepish, shy, and even a bit servile
We can disown our duties and blame others for anything
Which locks us in stuckness and inertia with everything

If we hear ourselves say: "I don't care," "Screw you!" or "Whatever!"
Our Champ is defending us from future disappointments and failures
Any time we sabotage our long-term happiness and wellbeing
It is the Champ's simple logic: defending against the danger it's
perceiving

When not in danger, the Champ still tries to stop us from getting what
we *don't* want
Protecting us from threats—rejection, loneliness, hurt, and bully's taunts

But in doing so, it blocks us from getting what we *do* want: creativity
    and loving freely
Champ cannot manifest our dreams—for this, we need a connection
    felt deeply

Sometimes Champ might obsess about driving forward a project or
    plan
Giving up self-care to deliver victory—like a vengeful Batman
Yet without taking care of ourselves: body and mind
We can quickly burn out or become resigned

The feeling that we can't change things can be agony
Sometimes the way forward is to accept this loss of agency
The Champ must sometimes surrender their need to win
To unlock trust, inspiration, and momentum

We have a right to feel angry when things seem unjust
The Champ's fire can help guide us to wrongness adjust
But without wisdom and heart, it will poison our days
Robbing us of true power and our entire spectrum of sun rays

Without softness within, the Champ will erect walls of steel
To keep out people that we think hurt, bully, or steal
If we allow this front to keep people out forever
We will struggle to love, be loved, and enjoy community endeavors

The key to taming the Champion is to remember that *we're already
    enough*
Because we're completed whole diamonds; even if in the rough
So we can play full out to compete and rise to each challenge
Trusting in our wholeness, divinity, and unique talents

WAYS TO AWAKEN THE WISDOM OF THE CHAMPION

The following are simple practices and exercises you can try out in your own space and time. They are not meant to replace professional support and are purely educational in their intent.

REFLECTING

Over the next few days, pay attention to how you react in difficult or stressful moments and write them down somewhere safe.

After a week or so, take a fresh piece of paper and draw two lines down the page to form three columns of roughly equal width. In the left-hand column, write down a list of all the ways you react when you feel upset, angry, or fearful. For example: defensive, arrogant, dismissive, withdrawing, people-pleasing, passive-aggressive, raging, or cynical.

Next to each one, in the middle column, write down how each behavior 'pattern' protects you from perceived threats to your physical, emotional, and social safety. Add in what you gain in terms of security and power.

Finally, in the right-hand column, write down what this behavior 'pattern' costs you in terms of connection, vulnerability, receptivity, authenticity, calm, confidence, creativity, and flexibility.

TALKING

'Interview' your friends, family, and intimate partner(s) for how you seem when you are upset triggered, destabilized, or defended. Add these to your list above.

Ask them how your strength and power—being committed, courageous, dependable, resilient, and loyal—positively impacts them.

Then ask them if there are moments when they would appreciate you being more courageous, empowered, and go-getting . . . or less competitive, aggressive, or avoidant.

APPRECIATING

Speak to the Champion in you directly, saying: "Thank you for always looking out for me. Thank you for defending me when nobody else would. Thank you for protecting me from dangers and threats, even when I have not always appreciated it. I am sorry I have not always appreciated you or supported you. Please forgive me."

Repeat this sentence until you find the Champion listening within. Allow any emotions, feelings, and sensations to move through you as you express complete gratitude for the Champion within you. If you don't feel anything, you may not be ready for this practice.

INVOKING

Speak to the Champion in you directly, saying: "I am ready for you to help me stand up strong in all situations with limitless courage, impeccable honor, and unbreakable resilience. I invoke you to fill my mind and body with the noble courage of the Champion."

Repeat this sentence until you find the Champion listening within. Allow any emotions, feelings, and sensations to move through you as you invoke the Champion within you to wake up and rise up. If you don't feel anything, you may not be ready for this practice.

INVITING

Ask your Champion: "What inner emotional or psychological support do you need from me to show up with more integrity, confidence, dependability, and courage?"

Keep asking this part of you and listen deeply for what arises.

Ask your Champion: "What inner emotional or psychological support do you need from me to be less defensive when I am not really being threatened—and so more open to new experiences, such as intimacy, imagination, and sensitivity?"

Keep asking this part of you and listen deeply for what arises.

TRANSFORMING

Take a few long, deep breaths, exhaling slowly without force. Focus your attention below your head, and scan from your neck to your pelvic floor, looking for where you feel most courageous and steadfast in your body. Choose to amplify any sensations that feel grounded and strong.

Now scan from your neck to your pelvic floor, looking for where you feel most afraid and unsteady in your body. Invite your Champion to fill up these spaces with its strength, determination, and power.

Now scan from your neck to your pelvic floor, seeking the places where you feel most angry, withdrawn, frozen, or overly defensive in your body. Breathe these sensations out from your mind and body with three deep exhales, saying to your Champion, "We don't need these habits as much anymore."

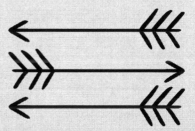

THE BOOK OF THE COMMANDER

MAKING ORDER FROM CHAOS

Within us all—no matter who—is a force of astonishing analysis and
    structure
A super-hero that will injustice, delusion, and foolishness rupture
This is the Commander; finding truth, answers, and ways to order
the complexities of life—and constrain chaos with borders

From our earliest years, we witness chaos and crazy
Messed-up situations—and ideas that are hazy
We invoke the Commander to pierce through the clouds
And seek what is honest and true in the maddening crowd

The Commander will ensure that we learn what's right
Decode the facts and push through to what's bright
Create order from chaos and spot patterns in nature
Bring harmony to discord and justice in life's legislature

Commander can look at all theories, ideas, and social media posts
Seeking veracity and factuality within lies, angles, and half-truths
We can take multiple perspectives and critically think
The wild claims of others then we judiciously shrink

Commander dedicates each moment to seeking and serving the truth
As wise folk have stated: truth is beauty and freedom. We get to
    choose!
Integrity and intellect are the Commander's prime tasks
Without them, we'll get stuck in swamps—and behind death-masks

As Commander, we keep our sword of truth and justice sharp
To fight battles against oppression, meanness, and the Dark
Then we can withstand uncertainty, confusion, disorder, and chaos
And can use all we have—digging deep—to reorder Kaos to Kosmos

To summarize, we make sense of confusion—so progress can be made
Cutting through the nonsense and lies with our truth-giving blade
We bring meaning when we're puzzled—when other folk are lost
Bringing fierce veracity and hope to prevent all holocausts

BUILDING A MAP OF LIFE

Each Commander must build their own map for how to pilot
Us to a life which has a point—and is also a bit pirate
Yet wise kith and kin have laid down tracks that can guide us
And their insights and clues will be essential for growing truth inside us

First, as Commander, we must master a technical skill or two
And put in the time to practice and grasp all the rules
We must embody the best ideas those before us have learned
About how both we and society can thrive—with nobody getting burnt

So explore what tickles your curiosity—and inspires in you the most
    intrigue
Which ideas that bring a rush of energy to mind that beats fatigue
Follow the breadcrumbs of inspiring knowledge and wisdom
Clues that open up insights and excellent intellectual systems

No matter how tough the questions or scary the doubts
We penetrate the hidden order of things we care about
With discipline and discernment, we can push on to find rigor
Where most folk give up, we can push for intellectual splendor

We're not afraid to speak up and ask the dumb questions
In service of learning and liberating insights that freshen
We are constantly unashamedly growing our genius
Whatever the subject, we seek out the ingenious

It's a complex world in which we must constantly make sense
Of what's changing around us—and what's making us tense
If we fill up our time with busyness and distractions
Commander has nothing left to process with the magnificent light of
    attention

If we stop making sense of complexity—and processing our quandaries
    each day
We'll get stuck under layers of perplexity—under which minds can be
    slayed
It's time to penetrate through clouds of distortion and confusion
With the Commander's superpowers of reflection and elevation

MAKING PROGRESS HAPPEN

The Commander is a solver of even the knottiest issues
Bringing intellect and analysis to wherever life is misused
We push and push until we reach absolute rigor
Never settling with woolliness, we problem-solve with vigor

We adore figuring things out—and having flashes of genius
That lights fires in our mind—and sparks solutions between us
Our Commander builds systems, maps, and theories
That can push our species forward—with juicy intellectual berries

The Commander learns tools to critique any idea or belief
That someone is peddling—even ourselves!—for their power and relief
Many cling on to outdated notions that offer comfort and convenience
But this Wizard within knows the truth of what's genuine genius

With science and reason, we might return to all citizens their dignity
Resolve wicked problems—that bring suffering—with mental acuity
The result is that justice is served to all those who oppress
Which moves humankind forward to the next stage of progress

Sometimes the 5% do inflict stark prejudice and abuse
The authorities fail to bring justice—the judges do snooze
Then wisdom whispers that the ultimate truth
Is to find peace with the indignities; and inside us soothe

As we gather the fruits from the tree of all knowledge
The shared data of humankind we appreciate, honor, and acknowledge
Then, with intellect firing, we can challenge all conventions and
    assumptions
And see if we can build what comes next with both humility and gumption

To ensure we have the energy needed for such contemplation and
    brilliance
We use structure, discipline, and routine to build unbreakable resilience
Then we can focus our attention on breaking through the limits
That lock human beings in—and our freedom inhibit

THE COMMANDER'S WEAK SPOTS

If our Commander is underdeveloped, weak, and small
We will be allergic to order, resulting in confusion for all
We'll get stuck in poor planning—and the resultant disorganization
May undermine our best intentions to deliver intelligence and
   innovation

An anemic Commander will make us phony—we'll even lie to ourselves
Condemning us to delusions and confusions in very dark realms
When we deceive others, we create the conditions for terrible abuse
No matter our protestations: to lie, there is never, ever an excuse

As the Commander, the truth-seeker, our word must be our bond
If we break it—or make lies up as will e go along
We have nothing to build on, no solidity or trust
And all noblest aspirations will likely turn to dust

As Commander, we are genius at truth, rigor, and order
Bringing harmony, dignity, justice—and clearly held borders
But when addicted to rigid structures, we can become hypercritical
Undermining the creativity of all by being relentlessly analytical

When we obsess about discipline, rigor, intellect, and technology
We cut ourselves off from our bodies, sensuality, and enlivening
   mythology
Even worse is the need to be always perfect and right
Which makes us arrogant—dismissing others—and their ideas, we
   might smite

We can be tempted to lose aliveness in the pursuit of perfection
Building masterful systems limited by their inhuman abstraction
The result is that we'll become lonely; lacking electrifying connections
Aloof, critical, and heartless will be other's perceptions

With too many routines, lists, and spreadsheets, we can't cope with
   uncertainty
This shuts down possibilities and life-changing spontaneity

We trade off creativity for a certainty that is usually an illusion
Our world will get smaller—circles decreasing— and we will get stuck
   in seclusion

The Commander can get obsessed with data and over-analysis
When we objectify others, we get stuck in relational paralysis
Time to wake up from scientific obsessions and control freakery
And bring back warmth and humility to our admirable geekery

Smarts can get us so far but then block us from going further
Something else is needed to cross over the widest river
This is to be wise, insightful, and emotionally intelligent
Understanding relationships brings us true elegance

Wit and intellect are useful to cut, parry, and thrust
But they tire everyone out, including ourselves!
So we watch out for sharp words—and pointing the finger
Embracing others for their differences—taking off our blinkers

One sign that we're lost in delusion is to be constantly cynical
And judge others—and their excitement—as boring and mythical
Such criticisms are simply a signal of loss
Of belief in ourselves and our own special sauce

We watch out for the trap of thinking, "I am (or they are) always so
   dumb"
These global beliefs lead us to feel lost, angry, and numb
We must never forget to turn the light of intellect back upon us
To question our motives and discern our blind spots

Self-awareness allows us to return to the mind of a beginner
Where we learn from everyone—best of all, their most vulnerable inner
We remember that being humble is the essence of progress
And the only way for all our super-powers to fully express

WAYS TO AWAKEN THE WISDOM
OF THE COMMANDER

The following are simple practices and exercises you can try out in your own space and time. They are not meant to replace professional support and are purely educational in their intent.

REFLECTING

Take some time to make sense of your life by looking at how different events have opened new opportunities, even if they appeared at the time to be negative or stressful. For example, changing schools enabled you to meet new friends, or having an illness gave you time to understand yourself better and develop new skills.

For a week, identify three things that go better than you expected them to, no matter how seemingly ordinary those things are.

TALKING

'Interview' your friends, family, and intimate partners about how your intelligence, organizing skills, and commitment to details positively impact them.

Then ask them if there are moments when they would appreciate you being more organized, honest, and discerning . . . or less controlling, choosy, or uptight.

APPRECIATING

Speak to the Commander in you directly, saying: "Thank you for being smart, truthful, rigorous, and structured, even when I have not always appreciated it. I am sorry I have not always appreciated you or supported you. Please forgive me."

Repeat this sentence until you find the Commander listening within. Allow any emotions, feelings, and sensations to move through you as you express complete gratitude for the Commander. If you don't feel anything, you may not be ready right now for this practice.

INVOKING

Speak to the Commander in you directly, saying: "I am ready for you to help me find the truth in all situations with lucid clarity, discerning intelligence, and brilliant decisiveness. I invoke you to fill my mind and body with the noble truth of the Commander."

Repeat this sentence until you find the Commander listening within. Allow any emotions, feelings, and sensations to move through you as you invoke the Commander within you to wake up and rise up. If you don't feel anything, you may not be ready right now for this practice.

INVITING

Ask your Commander: "What inner emotional or psychological support do you need from me to be less controlling or uptight?"

Keep asking this part of you and listen deeply for what arises.

Ask your Commander: "What inner emotional or psychological support do you need from me to be more organized and structured?"

Keep asking this part of you and listen deeply for what arises.

TRANSFORMING

Take some long deep breaths, exhaling slowly without force. Focus your attention below your head, and scan from your neck to your pelvic floor, looking for where you feel most truthful, bright, and discerning in your body. Choose to amplify any sensations that feel honest and insightful.

Now scan your neck to your pelvic floor, and find where you feel most disorganized, lacking truth, and chaotic. Invite your Commander to fill up these spaces with its capacity for harmony, order, and structure.

Now scan your neck to your pelvic floor, looking for where you feel most controlling, rigid, ruminative, and manipulative. Breathe these sensations out from your mind and body with three deep exhales, saying to your Commander, "We don't need these habits as much anymore."

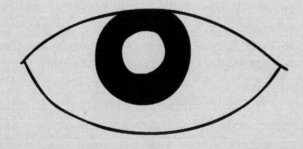

THE CREATIVE SPARK

Within us all—no matter who—is a force of glorious creativity
A super-hero that can solve novel problems with unprecedented
    activities
Our imaginative visions will unleash endless ideas that are fertile
With new possibilities that generate hope for a world that sparkles

Building upon intuition comes insight into others
From such empathy, we can solve problems that bother
Imagination and inventions bubble up from within us
From insights into humankind that dissolve what's unjust

We feel the movement of creativity in our bodies and then follow its
    lure
Creating new ways forward is a blues-breaking cure
As we open our senses to all life's insane riches
We can listen intently to our inspiring hunches

This Creator within us opens worlds that shimmer
With solutions and innovations that ways forward glimmer
This is not something we must do alone
To co-create with others is a life-changing boon

The Creator knows that it's our minds that block the insights and ideas
That are required to unleash new possibilities (after the tears)
Journeying from head to heart is no mean feat
For those of us brought up to prioritize being intelligent and elite

Without heart-awakening, we will endlessly get stuck
In the mirrors of the mind within which our egos run amok
Intelligence is necessary but not sufficient for artistry
It is creativity that breaks through unnecessary scarcity

We can bring this capacity for imagination, design, and creativity
Gifting to friends, communities, and organizations our generativity
We think nothing of starting a passion project today
That might make a better tomorrow and allow others to play

If we forge ideas within our inner diamantine quartz
With our imagination in the flowing water sourced
Then we flourish in hardship, whatever its nature
Learning and growing—our fulfillment we nurture

As Creator, we're fecund: ideas and inventions will stream
We never stop innovating and generating, having a dream
We can bring beauty to sadness, and aliveness to death
We can envision futures—and bring them to life with our breath

CREATING WITH CHALLENGES

Whenever we get blocked, upset, or hurt
There are always three ways to deal with problems that disconcert
We can repress our feelings; or react with rage
Neither of these works well as a way to a luminous Golden Age

The third path takes our imagination and agility
To take whatever happens and then respond to it with creativity
This is the path of embracing all that happens, whether in middle age or
     youth
And use it to unfold more love, possibility, and truth

We invoke our inner Creator to thrive, not despite
our troubles, trials, and tragedies that all lives blight
Things may not happen for any discernible reason
But Creator can use them to help our capacities to deepen

Life will offer many struggles and antagonists
Just enough to clarify our nature as the protagonist
In life's darkest moments, our character is revealed
If we can surrender our ego and to our wisdom yield

Life is full of chaos, discomfort, and cracks
We need these to shake us out of situations that are mismatched
If we trust that all our beliefs and habits can be transformed
There is always hope for a future that is less rubbed and worn

We say "yes" to all that is—but we are not fooled
Once we accept what is present, what becomes so cool
Is that we can choose to say "and" . . . then change what hurts, traps,
     and confines
Being guided to fruition by constantly arising signs

In this way, we can build bold and brace innovations
That solve needs better than the historical conventions
We can invent our way out of any tight spot
Never being satisfied with a mediocre lot

Rather than bitching and moaning about the stuff that frustrates
The only worthwhile response is to create
Try the unexplored and the untested—enliven!
Push the status quo to a brighter horizon

Instead of complaining about what is wrong with the world
We know better and invite ourselves to innovate and unfold
Rather than dread or denounce the dark—we light a candle with a
    vision
And make our ideas happen by harnessing creative frisson

CHANGING OURSELVES

Before we change the world with our inventor's vision
We must first change ourselves so we don't create fission
It is easy to see what others should do and how others must change
But the change we want to see begins with liberation from our own
    cage

Thus, the Creator is tasked with the most challenging of tasks
Changing ourselves and ripping off all remaining masks
It matters not how smart, bright, or ordered we are
If we cannot change ourselves, we are lost to interminable war

The Creator knows that changing ourselves only starts
When we are humble and give up being always so smart
We must first let go of old patterns that once served as our protection
But now keep us locked in traps and crushing deception

None of us gets to choose the challenges we must face
But we always get a choice to respond with imaginative grace
In *every* life, pain is inevitable, challenging, and very real
But suffering is optional—it's up to us how we deal

Even if we have been hurt early by life's harsh challenges
We must never forget that all trauma and pain can be metabolized
We can use the Creator's capacity to fire up a crucible
Within which we can melt down all angst into something usable

As an artist in life, we trust that in our deepest core
All pain can be transmuted by walking through our own heart's door
Our minds can make sense of confusion and struggle
But it is our hearts that must awaken if we want to artistically juggle

The Creator can work with whatever is happening
First own it, and embrace it, no matter how initially baffling
All change has its risks, which the Creator can tolerate
Because to avoid growth and change is to be dominated

By opening ourselves up to creativity, imaginative blossoms bloom
Then we can transform all wounds into a generative inner womb
We can turn any pain or pattern into possibilities that yield
A million ways forward: a thousand flowers in the field

With Creator at heart, we can invent more goodness, possibility, and
    beauty
Find within dark holes of despair, rich and radiant rubies
We can bring life to what's dull and revel in our senses
Taste, smell, touch, listen—seeing through a variety of lenses

THE CREATOR'S WEAK SPOTS

Our Creator can get obsessed with being special, entitled
And assume our genius and ideas are somehow unrivaled
These hang-ups can make us airy and dreamy; a little delusional
Following ideas to the stars that are fantasy, not beautiful

We can get fixated on design, art, novelties, and newness
Which rob us of humility, commonality, and trueness
Sometimes, it is crucial to live a life that is ordinary
And be one with our tribe—rather than unique and fragmentary

Sometimes, the Creator gets trapped in imagining
A thousand ideas while our time we are squandering
We might start projects and start up businesses endlessly
And never stay the course of building one relentlessly

So, once we have a vision that feels true to our heart
It's time to commit to its delivery with our strength and smarts
While we never want to stop having ideas and bold dreams
It's crucial to make some real to have a life supreme

When we feel we want to make something perfect
And we cringe in shame because idealism we expect
We recall to ourselves that making mistakes is an irritant
But it's crucial for learning, growth, and creative experiment

The Creator, when lacking, can have us become passive and bored
Apathetic and nihilistic, we may lose the joy that is existence's reward
We may think everything is dull and a bit shit
And that the best way to happiness is to be permanently lit

Without the Creator inspired, we may find that others' success triggers
    envy
Or that we lose our passion and simmer in a jealous frenzy
Allergies to creativity leave us gloomy and lifeless
We get ground down, conform, and forget that Being is priceless

Time to invoke the Creator and lose the uniformity and complacency
Blast away the nihilism that has us wandering around aimlessly
We gather, then focus, our energies on the obstacles that make us blue
And celebrate the wins of others as we have our next breakthrough

WAYS TO AWAKEN THE WISDOM OF THE CREATOR

The following are simple practices and exercises you can try out in your own space and time. They are not meant to replace professional support and are purely educational in their intent.

REFLECTING

Take some time to spot where you are creative, original, and imaginative in an average day; for example, in cooking, the route you walk to college, planning for social events, creating romantic moments, or trying new moves out in a video game.

Explore where you want more inventiveness, creativity, and spontaneity in your everyday life.

TALKING

'Interview' your friends, family, and intimate partners about how your imagination, originality, and creativity positively impact them.

Then ask them if there are any moments when they would appreciate you being more creative, flexible, and energized . . . or less innovative, explorative, or artistic.

APPRECIATING

Speak to the Creator in you directly, saying: "Thank you for being inventive, visionary, and imaginative, even when I have not always appreciated it. I am sorry I have not always appreciated you or supported you. Please forgive me."

Repeat this sentence until you find the Creator listening within. Allow any emotions, feelings, and sensations to move through you as you express complete gratitude for the Creator. If you don't feel anything, you may not be ready right now for this practice.

INVOKING

Speak to the Creator in you directly, saying: "I am ready for you to help me be creative in all situations with limitless curiosity, enlivening originality, and optimistic enthusiasm. I invoke you to fill my mind and body with the noble creativity of the Creator."

Repeat this sentence until you find the Creator listening within. Allow any emotions, feelings, and sensations to move through you as you invoke the Creator within you to wake up and rise up. If you don't feel anything, you may not be ready right now for this practice

INVITING

Ask your Creator: "What inner emotional or psychological support do you need from me to be less apathetic or static?"

Keep asking this part of you and listen deeply for what arises.

Ask your Creator: "What inner emotional or psychological support do you need from me to be more inventive and imaginative?"

Keep asking this part of you and listen deeply for what arises.

TRANSFORMING

Take a few long deep breaths, exhaling slowly without force. Focus your attention below your head, and scan from your neck to your pelvic floor to find where you feel most creative and imaginative.

Choose to amplify any sensations that feel inventive, enlivening, and full of possibility.

Now scan from your neck to your pelvic floor, looking for where in your body you feel most dull and conforming. Invite your Creator to fill up these spaces with its energy, liveliness, and originality.

Now scan from your neck to your pelvic floor, looking for where in your body you feel most entitled, daydreamy, and fantastical. Breathe these sensations out from your mind and body with three deep exhales, saying to your Creator, "We don't need these habits as much anymore."

THE BOOK OF THE CONNECTOR

WHO CARES WINS

Within us all—no matter who—is a force of limitless love
A super-hero that brings togetherness, healing, and the peace of the dove
The Connector will guide all to friendship, trust, belonging, and purpose
Who can always bring joy, passion, and affection to the surface

It's critical for any person of power and light
To navigate friendships, parents, and all social slights
We must find our truth, values, and direction
Yet stay bonded to friends and family in a dynamic connection

The Connector takes the time to be present to those we care for
Once we practice finding relationship resonance, it is no chore
Harmony can be found with almost anyone we meet
Enjoying their dance without treading on their feet

Romance, partnership, and intimacy beckon
Inviting our Connector to upgrade and quicken
We can now step into being a holistic lover
With journeys together and alone, to discover

When we find ourselves wondering, 'How best to fit in?'
With folk whom we like—but don't feel like our kin
The Connector will help us discern who is worth investing in
The folk that inspire our best side and open up win-win-wins

The Champion, Commander, and Creator can get seduced by their
    projects
The Connector knows that on relationships and connectivity, all life
    depends
Without intimacy and affinity, nothing great can be achieved
We need collaboration and partnership for opportunities to be seized

Our Connector knows all relationships take work: inspiring solidarity
The trick is to belong; without losing our singularity
The Connector favors listening over shouting; caring over solving
Empathizing with compassion, and our character evolving

With the Connector switched on, we can resonate with most

Even those who seem scary; and those who do us roast

The Connector says, "Everyone wants, in their deepest hearts, to be open"

It will welcome all people, no matter how frozen

BECOMING WHOLE

Whenever we feel we can't cope or are broken
Remember that everything in life can be a clue, a token
That fragments of us want to come back together
Once we choose in our heart to claim the Connector's tether

When we fight, judge, dismiss, or sit in fear of others
It's usually because of pain from insecure attachment to mothers,
    fathers, and brothers
Thus each moment of despair is the Connector's invitation to go inside
    to tend
To a field of relating that has become fragile and bent

We can release all our pain, and any wounds or damage heal
By connecting with something bigger than our egos, with zeal
This is nothing to do with religion, cults, or gods
It's about finding the love light within our biological bods

The Connector is waiting for us to call it and invoke
The magic, compassion, and loving-kindness that it evokes
We can use then use this loving liquidity to dissolve the hurts that still
    hinder
And cause us to be fake, false, fearful, or have flaming tinder

All the habits and actions that get us in trouble
Are there to defend us from more pain—acting like a protective bubble
So to break through self-sabotage, we must find the emotions that still
    hurt
And in the Connector's internal safe space, feel emotions and allow
    them to depart

The Connector allows us to have emotions but not be had by them
To have distance from pain but never become numb
The Connector knows there's a vast difference between feeling X
    versus being X
It allows feelings to pass because we don't let ourselves become
    vexed

Some of our pain may be from abuse, neglect, or trauma from our
ancestors
Some of it may be from bullying, break ups, or from those 5% of Death
Eaters
Everyone has wounds, and it matters not the cause
All can be released into peace when we breathe . . . and pause

A starting point is to start listening to our bodies: tracks feelings of
sorrow and shame
Then let the darkness be felt— within the safety of the Connector's
warm flame
It is in this inner ocean of love that all fear and rage can be
extinguished
Which allows all wounds to be repaired and all pain relinquished

Every dark night of the soul can be coped with in future
And no bruise, split, or gash need remain unsutured
It can seem like endless grief keep coming; a galaxy of sorrow
But the Connector breathes it away to create a luminescent tomorrow

We honor the Connector's soft and cyclical power to care
And truly become whole in ourselves—and have the freedom to share
This oceanic love inside can heal anything: from trauma to protective
shields
With compassion and love, we can cultivate limitless yields

With each upgrade into wholeness, we must leave old parts of us behind
That were once useful but now hold us back from being aligned
We can transform habits and wounds in the morning, noon, or night
This is the sole path to being whole, happy, and free—upright.

So, where we feel like we're in an emotional emergency
It's an invitation to heal within—with some urgency
It's time to switch on inside: light the fire of the Connector
And repair the schisms inside us: dissolve all haunting Specters

If the healing ever feels too hard—which it may well sometimes
We can say these Hawaiian words to ourselves in whispering rhymes
"Thank you. I love you. I'm sorry; please forgive me.
Help me, guide me; I'm ready to be free."

FINDING DEEP CONNECTION

When we feel upset, tense, empty, or numb
Anxious, withdrawing, despairing, or glum
It is the moment to breathe, relax, and release
Into the love within—all turmoil does cease

Nature, meditation, mentors, some medicine, and wisdom teachers
Can help us realize that we are pure love—in the form of a creature
By practicing ways to access self-love within the pain
We find that it's the only thing bigger than the sorrow and shame

"We are all one" is the most vital of realizations
The source of enlightenment and true liberation
The Connector murmurs, "You are the universe, conscious of its own
   evolution.
You can co-create with nature a spacious solution."

"You are a rock, a leaf, a drop of rain, a wheel spinning
A tiger, pencil, baby, your mortal enemy, and Guan Yin
You are the jewel within; the alpha and the omega terminal"
With this realization, all loss, grief, and pain become workable

Into this non-duality—some call it 'oneness'—we can our ego surrender
And swap out our Small Self for vastness, infinitude, and splendor
But to get such liberation, we must find our way to our heart's inner
   vault
When we do, we will feel like we've enjoyed a mystical somersault

As we journey within to find the spark of our life force
And discover our oneness—that we are all children of a loving cosmos
We can sense various flavors of unified consciousness
All can be practiced daily for a limitless renaissance

One flavor comes from deep breathing—a shimmering blue light
It helps us feel calm and clear, spacious and bright
We can reach it through silence and practicing meditation
Quieting our egos, this refuge brings us into connection

Another flavor expands our hearts, guts, and chests
A smoldering red resonance brings a sense of fullness
We can reach it through movement, chanting, and dance
We burn off our egos and enter a generative trance

The third flavor is the purple path of everyday tantra
"Find love for *everything*," is its devotional mantra
We can reach it by feeling passion for all things mundane
Tapping into a sensual joy to blast through the pain

Then there is the brown path of bowing heads to the earth
Connecting with trees, bees, and fungi affords us a daily rebirth
We can reach in through Nature and her humble dirt
We relax our minds and hearts as to the land we revert

These are all long-proven ways to transform troubles and suffering
And release hurts into an ocean of effervescent wondering
In this truth, wounds heal to become hard-won scars of wisdom
Its life's greatest lesson to trust in this intelligent system

Whichever paths and practices we take and make
The lesson from the Connector is to choose to awake
And feel loved by the universe—wanted, invited, and needed
All the answers we want lie waiting within: dormant and seeded

In the silence of contemplation or the dance of ecstasy, we can find our
    serenity
An emptiness—or fullness—that vanquishes all demons and enemies
As our hearts break, the cracks let in loving light
That shines through our bodies and out into the night

Hope is always at hand when we connect to the oneness within
The Connector will bring us back to nature's Earthy yin
Rewilding in nature—sea, forest, air—is the simplest way
To feel reverence in our chests until the end of our days

If we listen, the Connector whispers that the most incredible bliss resides
In surrendering our ego to connection, which is a better guide
It is only this awakening of unity by each of us super-heroes
That will ensure we never feel ourselves becoming zeroes

At all times, this garden of Eden inside us needs tending and mending
If we want to enjoy flowers all year and not by weeds be upended
Whenever we experience ourselves as fragmented, a lost soul
It means the Connector needs inviting to play its superhero role

THE CONNECTOR'S WEAK SPOTS

Our Connector is a genius at wholeness, compassion, and trust
We can be present, heartfelt, and belong—life's rarest gold dust
But a Connector that is obsessed with pleasures outside of them
May get addicted to food, feelings, and constant fornication

A Connector that is off-kilter can become overly enmeshed
Finding it hard to separate, always full of neediness
We can be gossipy, dramatic; in others' business too involved
Finding our boundaries and confidence endlessly dissolved

To love others fully, our Connector must be vulnerable and sensitive
But if it collapses inside to please others, it's never generative
Caring, compassionate, kind but never fawningly soft
Otherwise, moody and melodramatic, Connector gets lost

A blurry Connector can think our happiness (or anger) is caused by
     others
So we must never abscond from our true colors
There is no value in people-pleasing, co-dependence, or fawning
They all stop us from being with others in authentic belonging

An absent Connector will be aloof, lonely, and guarded
Withdrawing from the group and running away—close-hearted
If our Connector was hurt, we might cope by going quite numb
Which will have us downcast and constantly glum

By sparking ourselves with nature, love, and connection
We can awaken our hearts with a healthy affection
This allows us to melt what is frozen and frigid
Loosening us up, we become less stuck and rigid

If we find a cold Connector stopping the flow of generosity
That spills out from healed hearts with glorious ferocity
Give and give more, and don't stop caring
A life well-lived is centered on sharing

Watch for minutes and moments that from our bodies, our Connector
   dissociates us
When we leave our feeling and senses, our consciousness is concussed
Nothing other than love can heal splinters in our being
Fighting, fleeing, fawning, or fornicating will never set us free

Sometimes a lost and lacking Connector gets rapaciously hungry
And seeks nourishing belonging in a cult, club, clique, or country
These are just proxies for the love and acceptance we all yearn for
Only the Connector's electric love can ensure our spirits always soar

WAYS TO AWAKEN THE WISDOM OF THE CONNECTOR

The following are simple practices and exercises you can try out in your own space and time. They are not meant to replace professional support and are purely educational in their intent.

REFLECTING

Take some time to spot how you already find moments of peace, quietness, connection, slowness, and contemplation in a day, e.g., walking the dog, running, being in nature, doing a chore quietly.

Explore what you might do to find more moments of contemplation and connection. Consider starting a form of meditation, relaxation, martial art, or movement practice for connection.

TALKING

'Interview' your friends, family, and intimate partners for how your openness, care, generosity, vulnerability, love, and friendship positively impact them.

Then ask them if there are moments when they would appreciate you being less concerned about them.

APPRECIATING

Speak to the Connector in you directly, saying: "Thank you for being caring, generous, loving, and compassionate, even when I have not always appreciated it. I am sorry I have not always appreciated you or supported you. Please forgive me."

Repeat this sentence until you find the Connector listening within. Allow any emotions, feelings, and sensations to move through you as you express complete gratitude for the Connector. If you don't feel anything, you may not be ready right now for this practice.

INVOKING

Speak to the Connector in you directly, saying: "I am ready for you to help me feel love in all situations with abundant compassion, deep intuition, and caring sensitivity. I invoke you to fill my mind and body with the noble love of the Connector."

Repeat this sentence until you find the Connector listening within. Allow any emotions, feelings, and sensations to move through you as you invoke the Connector within you to wake up and rise up. If you don't feel anything, you may not be ready right now for this practice.

INVITING

Ask your Connector: "What inner emotional or psychological support do you need from me to be more loving, kind, wise, and compassionate?"

Keep asking this part of you and listen deeply for what arises.

Ask your Connector: "What inner emotional or psychological support do you need from me to be less co-dependent, melodramatic, and bothered by what other people say or do?"

Keep asking this part of you and listen deeply for what arises.

TRANSFORMING

Take some long deep breaths, exhaling slowly without force. Focus your attention below your head, and scan from your neck to your pelvic floor, looking for where you feel most connected, empathic, and loving in your body. Choose to amplify any sensations that feel caring, heartfelt, and compassionate.

Now scan from your neck to your pelvic floor, looking for where in your body you feel most numb, isolated, and cold. Invite your Connector to fill these spaces with passion, warmth, and kindness.

Now scan from your neck to your pelvic floor, looking for where in your body you feel most needy and moody. Breathe these sensations out from your mind and body with three deep exhales, saying to your Connector, "We don't need these habits as much anymore."

PART 3

BECOMING A LEADER
IN YOUR OWN LIFE

EVERYDAY LEADERS BALANCE THE FOUR ELEMENTALS

Four ways of seeing we have by dint of being alive
The Connector helps us love; the Champion ensures we survive
The Commander solves problems and orders the clutter
While the Creator imagines new ways to forge a better future

The Champion protects us from dangers with defensive strategies
The Connector guides us with intuition and ensures we thrive in families
The Commander cuts through the confusion and allows us to
     understand what was meant
The Creator comes up with ideas when we need to reinvent

We now have a Council of Elementals to offer up solutions
To any problem that we face—there are four forceful resolutions
Ask each Elemental, in turn, what path it suggests
To have a breakthrough listen to its requests

Champion and Commander alone may seem all-powerful
But without kindness and creativity, our swords become brittle
Strength and wits that are not sourced in sensitivity and softness
Can lead directly to bleakness, burnout, and infinite brokenness

While Champion and Commander are inspired by masculine (not male)
     genius
Generating algorithms, straight lines, and productivity: ingenious
The Creator and Connector come from a force more feminine
That is receptive, compassionate, and always genuine

The Champion's force is softened by the Connector's open and warm
     heart
So we're inspired to fight for things good—that which elevates and
     supports
The Commander ensures that the love is not wish-washy and weak
By using our intellect to drive us to the top of a peak

The Commander embraces confusion to see a way through complexity
And grounds the Connector's passion in distanced equanimity
The Creator brings fresh thinking, ideas, and imagination
Ensuring the Commander's analysis is alive and unlocks elation

The Connector grounds all we do in purpose and caring
So the Champion wins wars in which the spoils are for sharing
So the Commander never loses alliances because of sheer arrogance
So the Creator doesn't get lost in ideas that end in horridness

The Champion limits love to stop enmeshment and self-neglect
The Commander focuses the love on making sure it has an effect
The Creator ensures that this love turns into imaginative solutions
Thus, the Connector can pour into our world to deliver wisdom
    revolutions

The Champion and Commander are far better at stopping
Us from getting what we fear: being hurt again or in chaos be dropped in
For it is the Connector and Creator who most generate our heart's
    longing
A life of meaning, ideas, happiness, love, and true belonging

Our society's great blind spot is the role of the Creator and Connector
Rewarding pride, profit, and productivity over love's rarified nectar
Educations and enterprises rarely spark reward Connector or Creator
Filling minds with facts instead of inspiring imaginations greater

Word to the wise: invest time in your creativity and wholeness
Find creativity, self-healing, and interdependent closeness
The Creator and Connector are unlockers of a life full of flourishing
Once they are reclaimed, every day will be life-affirming and
    encouraging!

Each of these four super-heroes you now have access to
The four characters, four corners, four Elementals
They now come together in the form of a single Leader
One who has integrated each part and become a wisdom keeper

STEPPING UP AS A LEADER

Every one of us has a choice: to heed the call of the Hero
Which requires listening to our hearts—and following the flight of
    truth's arrow
We can be both wise and wild, claiming all that life has to offer
Says this humble, caring, and adoring father

As true leaders, we get to craft our own epic tales
Activating and invoking all four prime Elementals
Every challenge we face becomes a clear invitation
To unlock more super-strengths and power-ups hasten

When the leader has risen, we can break through any of life's
    challenges
That all of us will face as we encounter dangers and damages
Like how to feel happy when there seems to be little to shout about
When we feel hurt, angry, or broken—despairing and full of doubt

It is tempting to try to disappear from life's complications
By avoiding people, problems, and stressful occasions
This may work for a while to keep the darkness at bay
But our life will get so small it will hurt in its own way

We may try to use addictions to escape all shades of blue
But it won't work for long and will cause endless doo doo
We may get caught in criminal traps and menacing evils
Putting us in real danger, which can be lethal

If we find ourselves escaping with pills and thrills
Or getting addicted to things that seek to emptiness fill
Remember, nothing outside us can provide the love we need
It waits in our hearts to be by the Connector freed

All desires can be tricky and lead to addiction
Sex, work, tech, and stuff collecting—can all be an affliction
Our brain doesn't care whether we get 'it' or not
It's hooked on anticipating the next thing to be caught

Use the Connector to juice the insides and unleash eternal satisfaction
And calm impulses for 'me, mine, and more' that in our heads' klaxon
There is no way to escape the need for doing 'inner work'
By which we clear away all that blocks our unique creative spark

No experience of excitement will ever heal emotional wounds
That hurt and smart and spin us all around
It's a mistake to think things outside can fill holes
The only solution is to do the work to become ever more whole

This is why caring parents maintain strong (yet permeable) boundaries
   for their child's safety
Until brains develop strength and discernment, they'll be too hasty
Wise folks must lead their kids with firm membranes to keep out
   danger and death
While empowering their kids to become leaders with each conscious
   breath

The mature leader learns, often sadly, that we can't always have our
   own way
That boundaries give us honor and keep excesses at bay
Constraints set us free: it works to live within limits
But limitless, we can still feel every damn minute

As leaders, our challenges are how to have a life full of meaning
And to walk into any room with a sense of belonging
To feel confident, at peace, and by others appreciated
And be able to ensure our problems can be alleviated

I can't give all the answers, just some words of wise guidance
On learning, healing, careers plus purpose and self-reliance
I will also share some tips for sex, love, and dating
And how the best lives are full of meaningful relating

But before you take these words as biblical revelation
Remember that each leader must their own path blazon
Ask your own questions, and then answer them, too
All I can do is offer up these well-being and wisdom clues

LEADING OURSELVES TOWARDS WELLBEING & WISDOM

As a leader, we must take good care of our bodies and minds
If we don't want to be by stress and strains confined
We're no use to others if we're falling apart within
So we must take our self-care seriously; it is not hippy spin

Taking care of ourselves can be hard to fathom at the beginning
When going out, partying, and having adventures seems so thrilling
Loving ourselves and our bodies may seem to be a bit crap
Compared to gaming, TikTok, dating, and WhatsApp

But the importance of taking care of the body and mind
And those of others, through being each day kind
It cannot be overstated: it is the start of all goodness
The only way to ever achieve true happiness and fullness

To love our own body is the starting point for all thriving
We adore our bod as much as we do stars, beaches, and the sun rising
Every part of us is worthy of the love we might give a puppy
Whether, right now, we feel spotty, skinny, sweaty, or chubby

To keep the happiness flowing, we must invest in being healthy
With discipline and effort, this means using our muscles regularly
When looking in the mirror, choose to see all our bits as beauty
Appreciating each part of ourselves is our sworn duty

We must take time each week to process, reflect, and wonder
And once we have made sense of stress—make time to slumber
The starting point of happiness is getting decent sleep
As well as eating well, exercising, and maintaining our bodies' upkeep

Loving life and the world starts with tending to our cells
From which emerge our creativity and fun—like magic spells
The more we make healthful sleep, eating, and exercise a regular fixture
The more enjoyment can be had in our everyday mixture

Reason and science are the best way to be certain
About things outside us that minds can study and sharpen
Science, logic, and tech can shoot us to the stars
But they can also disconnect us and start painful wars

Many will have intelligence, information, and keenness
But our inner guru is the grokkiest genius
Its intuition is not the same as noisy, defensive instinct
Intuition is quiet, subtle, life-bringing—yet always persistent

We may have been taught that all knowledge can be learned
But leaders discover quickly that wisdom comes from living—it must
    be earned!
If, as a leader, our efforts are sourced in a wise, juicy heart
We can always radiate hope—with both wisdom and smarts
As we expand our wisdom, we can transmute all fear to aliveness
And live at the edge of chaos while maintaining uprightness
Leaders know that we can always draw on our four super-powers
Sparkling ideas, courageous wisdom, and deep insight will flower

We can release whatever is not serving us into our heart's liquid light
And wake up whatever we need within to reach ever greater heights
But if we make the mistake of thinking that we are fixed in a certain way
Our deluded identity will block us until the end of our days

The leader seeks to integrate all Four Elementals—all seeming opposites
And resolve any tensions within us from our parents and inner conflicts
About matters of the heart, relationships, happiness, and meaning
Discerning wisdom ensures our bodies and minds stay beaming

LEADING OURSELVES TOWARDS HAPPINESS AND INNER PEACE

Many think the aim of life is to be cheerful and successful
But wisdom teaches us that to blossom in adversity is what's celestial
Many of our moments will be difficult and unpleasant: it's a fact
So thriving *because we grow through our problems* is the way to adapt

If a feeling of upset comes, we stay in our body: chest, heart, and gut
Starting right now—there's no better happiness shortcut
By finding something bigger than our egos to connect with
We can extinguish all anguish from our own inner Sith

Leaders don't fear pain, whether emotional or mental
We see it as a source of information for wholeness: instrumental!
We dare to follow all and any pain inside us to its original source

Where we will find clues that unlock, for us, the right course
When we feel disease or unease, we pause, reflect, and think:
Is it time for the Connector to let go and peacefulness drink?
Or is it time for the Champion to step up in breakthrough action?
Often both are the way to true life satisfaction!

The Champ helps us contain our anger and emotional charges
Self-regulated, the Commander makes sense of what within us surges
The Connector heals pain and soothes all nervous jitters
So the Creator can try a new way to respond to the triggers

Not all of life's challenges can be fully solved or with dealt
Sometimes the wisdom is just to let them be felt
Once we give our body and mind permission to be with what is
It will do what is needed to return us to bliss

Occasionally, strong emotions may feel so intense
That we think we will be knocked over the fence
But they will pass if we dare to let them be there
And they will tell us things about what needs our highest care

Bittersweet moments will then quickly pass
And what may come next is a great big laugh!
We *must* grief—it can feel unbearable—but all sadness must be felt
Otherwise, it sticks around in our bodies and stops us from self-help

Painful memories and emotional wounds from our past: they're a
    feature, not a bug
We've evolved to avoid threats by remembering each blow and tug
Inner angst ensures we survive by staying away: fight or flight
But without choosing to process it, we'll be stuck in stressful nights

If sadness, anger, or worry do wake us up in the night
It's a moment to feel, make sense of, and release the pain and the
    slights
Then we can transform all addictions, allergies, and desires that we feel
We can choose openness and tenderness—and, in the moment, heal

Pretty much all of our suffering can, like this, be changed
The more we transform the pain, the more we become in life engaged
Then we can love what we've lost; and what is within us least
And constantly allow all our pain to be released

Frankly, so much of life is so darn sad with each day's dawn
Moments, people, and love must all be waved gone
Leaders feel free to cry hot tears with the whole of our being
Sometimes it is the best way to find us some freeing

Grief for loss, love, adventure, youth, and opportunities
Of meaning and beliefs that we thought were certainties
Must be felt fully and completely to turn pain into peace
Then we can rise to thrive each day, and the troubles will cease

This means trusting that our heart—once full of the love of the
    Connector
Needs nothing beyond it—so it can then give endless self-affection
With blue, red, purple, and brown we can release patterns that are no
    longer serving
Which will bring us the real stuff that our inherent beauty is deserving

We can connect with the sorrow that hurts all hearts
Each of us has suffered from different causes, but all equally hurt
There is no point judging suffering as more or less than anyone else's
Compassion receives all pain and moves to resolve it

Living openly and honestly with constant transformation
May seem daunting and serious and full of consternation
But actually, it is the path to the most exciting adventures
As it beats any extreme sports, travel, or glamorous Avengers

But stay wary that, after each glorious expansion
Will likely come a surprisingly sharp and painful contraction
This happens when outdated habits snap back once again
As the Champ tries to protect us when it feels most vulnerable and Zen

Don't worry: this expansion and then contraction is the rhythm of life
We have to remember to reconnect once we feel inner strife
The Connector can soothe our Champ's fiery defenses
And guide us to keep growing and going with all our senses

Sometimes it may seem like there is endless suffering and sorrow
Wounds of ours, our parents, and our ancestors block a brighter
    tomorrow
But the Connector knows all pain can be felt and released
It will ensure we come back to our center. Now breathe!

Let us try not to make more tears than those that will flood
As we grieve for success, love, and joy that we've lost
Let's not sweat the small stuff and remember the love of our kin
Those who love us unconditionally are the rarest of things

LEADING OURSELVES TOWARDS GREAT FRIENDSHIPS

We must make an effort to nourish a supportive community
That can help us deal with stress and bounce back in unity
Nurture mentors, allies, and those who share the same path of freedom
Remember, we're in this together, with every breath taken

As we become adults in society, moving away from our folks
Friendships become essential, and in us, great things invoke
This need not mean our family can't be close to us too
We can have our cake and eat it—if we stay true

One piece of wisdom can be utterly liberating
For a lifetime of freedom from rejection and self-hating
We stop expecting everyone we like to like us
Some connections aren't a fit, and this ain't no cuss

Some people will inspire us to be more honorable and gentle
Some will trigger us to be dishonorable, dark, and temperamental
Some will bring forth the better angels of our nature
Some (like the 5%) will provoke cruelty and cowardice: our inner hater

It pays to invest in those few who are kind-hearted
Those who bring out our best and who won't shame us if we've farted
Keeping the rest a little distant, we help our hearts feel most whole
Holding a little back without trying to always be in control

No matter who we are, we are all worthy of love, honor, and care
Because we're the universe's kids—kind, noble and fair
We need never get lost in self-hatred or self-criticism
Because we can breathe our way back to our heart's love-light prism

When people say mean things aimed to put us down
We hold our heads up high with no need to frown
Such words say more about them than they do about us
No need to listen to them or let ourselves get cross

People say things when scared, small-minded, ignorant
Forgive them immediately, and don't get indignant
No need to give them our power by taking things personally
Yet always see if there are learnings from the lesson of life's university

Friends can be a source of peer pressure or peer power
It is all down to us and how we choose to flower
If we let fear of others influence how we act
We allow their hang-ups to make our joy contract

The opinions of others are theirs and just that
They may be helpful, but they may also be mere chat
Listen to their views; we take feedback on board
But we know we're always sovereign with our truthful sword

Lacking wisdom, we might struggle not to feel wronged
And fully heavily in love with gangs that make us feel strong
But if we don't want to get lost, we must go deeper within
To find the Connector's love which brings back our grin

Be warned: there are some people—say 5%—with whom we must
    always be on guard
Our Champion must keep firm boundaries to protect our heart's
    deepest parts
They don't mean to do it, but they thrive on the hurt of others
Bullying, shaming, manipulating; life and love snuffers

These Death Eaters must be contained; screening us from their venom
We can't let their internal trauma our body and mind poison
We can have compassion without taking on their toxins
Remembering our sovereignty and self-care is the best option

As a leader, we can always lay down boundaries that protect
We can keep violence, acidity, and deceit in check
Each border is there to keep integrity alive
But still porous to allow in others' perspectives, so we all thrive

Yet with Four Elementals balanced, we can see in all their wholeness
Treating them with decency and trust in the first instance
But if they betray, steal, or damage—we may need to say "Bye, bye"
View them with compassion but not on them rely

LEADING OURSELVES TOWARDS A SUPPORTIVE COMMUNITY

We must take care of the people we rely on for nourishment
Investing energy and effort into our community, even when we feel
  discouragement
For those we want to form the core of our empowering tribe
We must do things for them, even when it's a pain in the backside

Belonging is forged through both fun times and strange
Especially when we support each other to change
Life is sweetest when we see the best in others—and appreciate them
  freely
And calm our impulses to be manipulative, moany, or mealy

The more we invest in our community, the more trust fills the bank
Which we will spend in times of difficulty, stress, and rank
We build trust as currency by clearly appreciating others' gifts
Caring for them when they need us and working to heal all rifts

We can stretch to meet everyone in their superpowers and protective
  patterns
And be honest about our own, seeing where others withdraw from or
  flatten
One thing every human shares is that we all have our own 'stuff'
And it takes conversations to transcend it, both easy and tough

Everyone has their foibles; patterns they use to defend
Some people are fighters who get hot, speak out, but don't pretend
Some people flee—but also seem cold, offish, and passive
But are difficult to befriend; and no less aggressive

Leaders know that all clashes are creativity in disguise
We can all grow from the discord and become more loving inside
With all relationships, conflicts will happen and cause strife
This is a natural result of two different views on life

As leaders, we have no qualms about freely owning our 50%
Of what went wrong in a relationship: but we leave the rest to them
Our Connector will tell us to apologize wholeheartedly
Our Champion will ensure we don't take on what's theirs: this is artistry

To err is human, to forgive is divine
Reconciliation is a joyful thing to design
Fights will likely lead to harsh words and rupture
But rapid repair returns all involved to everyday rapture

Often what's needed is an honest and heartfelt apology
And listening deeply to others and learning from them, consciously
For any relationship to work, we must own our mistakes
We can be right or have a good relationship: this is what's at stake

If we avoid taking responsibility for our missteps and blunders
Others will avoid us in turn—they will have our number
For all the rights, liberties, and gifts we desire to see
Only arise with equal duties, cares, and responsibilities

Leaders build connection, community, and trustworthiness
Through reciprocity, honor, and a commitment to justice
As a leader, we learn how to freely give and give
The best of ourselves to our community; and how to always forgive

LEADING OURSELVES TOWARD LOVING RELATIONSHIPS

Intimacy is one of life's greatest gifts—and challenges!
It can turn us upside down and take us to our edges
Where we must trust, open, and share even when frightened
This is a path to becoming everyday enlightened

Luckily, most parents offer their kids unconditional love
This sets us up for closeness—some folks will fit like a glove
But some parents struggle to love without needing anything in return
We then find it difficult to know what love is and its truth discern

With resulting insecurity, we may hide behind a mask
Or try to 'win' the love of others: always an impossible task
As a leader, we know its time tend to the wounds within
If we want to attract kind lovers; and flames that feel like a twin

As a leader, we can be unashamedly passionate
Causing others to quiver—our love can be adamant
Yet always tender, thoughtful, and respectful are we
And above all, as faithful as a giant Redwood tree

There's never a need to be shy: everyone is in the same boat
No matter how cool people seem, all hearts can be smote
The worse anyone can say is 'no'—but we will keep the victory
Of having asked in the first place, opening up the possibility

We will meet lots of people who get our juices going
But far fewer will cause the love to start flowing
It may be tempting to rush in with a whirlwind of joy
It's better to slow down and take it easy: enjoy!

Leaders stay present, authentic and listen to others deeply
They don't promise anything until it feels right to love freely
Let's see if the other can handle our unique foibles and fragilities
Before we ready our beautiful bodies for full sexualities

Leaders find ways to love others without defensive walls
Which often requires the most profound healing of all
Then we never lose ourselves as we fall for a special one
We can be both island and ocean: interdependent

With love, lust, and sex, things can quickly get serious
Pregnancies, divorces, and abortions can be pretty deleterious
So, let's give our hearts time to open and unwind
Before we make promises that will to others, us bind

No matter their beauty, status, or sensual delight
To be honored, respected, and appreciated is our birthright
Both our bodies and hearts are precious and tender
Let's not give them away too quickly on a drunken bender

It may be tempting to think porn is somehow a reality
It can be fun, but it's a performance that soon becomes a banality
It's often far more violent than anyone real actually wants
And usually made by sex traffickers, pimps, and criminal establishments

True sensuality comes from opening our hearts
Touching, sensing, and kissing is the most genuine art
We come into union with the body of another
And so become a receptive and legendary lover

It's easy to get seduced by fantasies of perfection
And project onto others' incredible expectations
Nobody is a finished product; this is not the point of love matches
Instead, it seems to be about growing without giving each other too
    many deep scratches

On the path of true love, things will always get bumpy
Some say the point of romance is for each to become less clunky
To work on our patterns and problems: two distinct people, yet one
While not being needy, so we are always happy alone

Sometimes it's hard to know when to try harder or if it's burnt
Many relationships will be done when mutual lessons are learned
The point is not perfection but growth through vulnerability and play
Very few lovers can walk us to the end of our days

If we ever feel that we might cheat or can't stay the distance
Leaders share honorably and honestly our feelings of resistance
Whatever we do, we don't tell lies that all goodness corrodes
We speak our truth, even when scary, and share the load

This is when all our nobility and virtue most matter
So, we can show up as folk who never do shatter
The hearts of those we love—or burn any bridges
Integrity is the foundation for all love's riches

If we find one who is stellar and trustworthy in their heart
We can learn together, and the spark always seems to restart
We need to commit to them and close all the escape doors
And choose to come back, again and again, to love once more

In the crucible of commitment, most fears can be released
Leaders can love each other deeply as the years are increased
Nobody can promise they'll be there forever
A partnership must always be a rewarding endeavor

LEADING OURSELVES TOWARDS A MEANINGFUL CAREER

What will we do with our time as students, workers, or leaders?
What subjects should we study; what jobs make us eager?
Best we go deep and wide, trying a multitude of hobbies and subjects
Until we find what inspires us, whether simple or complex

We can't live someone else's life or do what makes others feel good
  cheer
We must stride on our own; and continue through the tears and fears
Wrong decisions will be made; leaders don't get disheartened
We keep moving forwards, releasing needless burdens

Experience has taught me that we all seem to have a career theme
That shows up when we're young; when we're confident to share our
  dreams
Our theme is not always apparent as it rarely fits the conventions
It's more of a set of magical moments that together capture our
  attention

Let us always take note of what lights us up; what sparks intrigue, and
  inspires
Is it working with our hands, moving, acting, science, or coding silicon
  wires?
Let's spend our youth discovering these incandescent bulbs of delight
And see how to knit them together in a career of unified light

As leaders, we choose our steppingstones wisely (but without anxiety
  or regrets)
The steps may only make total sense when looking back with 20/20
  specs
Following our theme but allowing serendipity to bring its gifts
Unpredictable opportunities—that seem to come out of nowhere—can
  our lives shift

Some say we need the Champ's diligence and discipline, across 10,000
    hours, to master
A technical skill or two that will our livelihoods look after
Our Commander learns, integrates, remembers, and stores
What we need to deliver on so our boss does us adore

It seems not to matter *exactly* want we end up working on
As long as it brings us deep meaning, fulfillment, and lots to learn from
Leaders do their best to deliver the utmost quality
Giving each task our all—whole heart and mind—with sovereignty

One of the secrets of fulfillment is to have total devotion
To bringing forth our dreams, aspirations, and passionate notions
By being dedicated to our work, every fiber of our soul
We can stop time slipping through our fingers before we do it know

There is a trick to fulfillment that comes from ancient sources
A way of living and leading that comes to use from a variety of verses
It is not to get hooked or attached to the fruits of our labor
And be equally at peace with failure or success—and that of our
    neighbors

Experts will tell us what has been helpful up until now to fly high
Yet most knowledge gets out of date; our Creator must surprise
But only once we have mastered some expertise should we challenge
    (with humility)
Rules that lock people into uniformity and outdated realities

As leaders, we blast through conventions: no longer conforming to
    others
Without thinking, we know it all—as much ancient wisdom matters
We are confident in our truth, without hubris or arrogance
We avoid foolishness—and our bullshit—with discerning intelligence

The sword of truth can be scary, as outdated ideas, it does kill
Whether wand, scepter, or shaft—we must temper their thrills
We need blades to get rid of what is old: things whose time is to die
Then we can forge, create, and imagine our way to the sky

It's easy to step back from where the action is real
By endlessly commenting from the edge of the field
It takes guts and conviction to step into the arena
Where we may fail or mess up—and get laughed at by Death Eaters

We must have lots of strength to share our frailties and fragilities
Which come into sharp relief on pathways of entrepreneurial
    possibilities
Our support network of friends and colleagues will be critical
As we start our projects—and aim at scary, hairy goals

There will always be others to collaborate on progressing further
Those who will stand by us—our sisters and brothers
As we embark on a journey together; on shared sailing ships
We can weather storms with the gift of fellowship

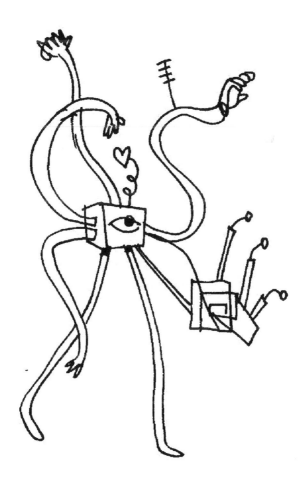

LEADING OURSELVES TOWARDS MAKING A DIFFERENCE

Wise leaders are rebellious yet not for their fame or gain
We're here to serve society, and so relieve some of the pain
We want to care for our planet and root our work in our Earth
Moving to tend to all others with love (and kindness, of course)

If we find ourselves asking, "Just what is the point?"
Of this life so challenging that it can knock us out of joint
I believe the purpose is to use our talents to serve a reduction of
    suffering
And do what we can to bring all around us into a state of greater
    flourishing

If we go forth into our beautiful yet dangerous world
Armed only with ambition and drive—we will find it so cold
We need something brighter, warmer, and loving to serve
With all our might, energy, and heartfelt verve

Some call this our 'purpose'; which is not some big, audacious goal
Our purpose is whatever makes us feel most whole
It is who we are when we love, lead, laugh, and learn the most
While generating a livelihood—which is crucial to toast

By being who we are when our heart is most caring yet free
We will become all we must be to bring to others to esprit
We each must follow our unique clues to discover our purpose
Which takes time to understand—and means giving up some
    convenience

We need not crack it now: just do more of what feels most heart-warming
That brings us the most joy, belonging, autonomy, and learning
Science has confirmed that those who live longer
Are those who find meaning over fame, fortune, and being a
    hatemonger

None get to choose what is their life's calling
Circumstances may have decided it—but it's always enthralling!
Yet we do get to choose what we do with our unique métier
And use it to alleviate the pain of others and make the world a wee bit
    better

There are many ways to be of service to others
Art, entertainment, education, entrepreneurship, and being a mother
Rather than waste energy fighting against confected enemies
We use our power to vanquish cruelty, climate change, and inequality

One thing to watch out for is that there is no greater agony
Than knowing our purpose but ignoring it to get money
So, leaders, watch out instead for the moments with the most meaning
And guide each day to bring more of this life-affirming greening

With practice, we can unleash love from our hearts and let it pour out
    into action
Serving others in some way we will find true satisfaction
Purposeful brilliance comes from a heart that is a little bit healed
Which takes time, patience, practice—and our ego to yield

Our Champion has the courage to deal with the discomfort and
    inconvenience
Of shifting our world to do what's right and live in a way that is
    seamless
Our Commander will propose a more harmonious and just order
Our Creator will invent solutions that remake the border

Yet, it's the Connector that grounds all we do in purpose
Ensuring our insights and ideas come out of love's furnace
Power to, not over, will prevent the demise
Of our planet and our people from sea levels that rise

All crises on Earth—from social media to pollution—we can soothe
When we balance the Four Elementals and find our own groove
We can love, be loved, make an impact—and learn all the time
As we shape our destiny to the sound of our rhymes

APPENDIX

THE FOUR ELEMENTALS OF
WISE LEADERSHIP

THE CHAMPION

SUPERPOWERS

Protective, disciplined, seeking-momentum, dignified, perseverant, bold, confident, productive, rooted, loyal, stable, robust, strong, successful, majestic, courageous, honorable, accountable, autonomous, ready-to-sacrifice, resolved, go-getting

ADDICTIONS

Adrenaline addict, hostile, rebellious, brutal, venal, aggressive, vengeful, conflictual, destructive, addicted-to-success, competitive, cut-throat, brittle, frenetic, selfish

ALLERGIES

Cowardly, indecisive, hesitant, doubtful, full-of-procrastination, weak, petulant, dependent, servile, defeatist, dominated, reluctant, discourageable, shy, irresponsible

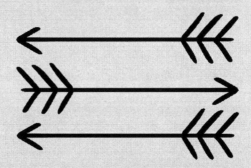

THE COMMANDER

SUPERPOWERS

Truthful, ordered, analytical, discerning, exceptional, reflective, intellectual, rigorous, structured, conscientiousness, figuring things out, perspective-taking, excellence, seeking explanations, progressive, just, systematic, systemic, diligent, masterful, skeptical, grounded

ADDICTIONS

Controlling, contemptuous, manipulative, deceitful, rigid, earnest, habitual, abstract, perfectionistic, dismissive, ruminative, arrogant, mechanical, prejudiced, cynical, self-righteous, pessimistic, driven by own agenda

ALLERGIES

Chaotic, confused, untruthful, unaware, misleading, exasperating, disorganized, undiscerning, second-rate, unjust, inappropriate, inaccurate, insincere, hypocritical

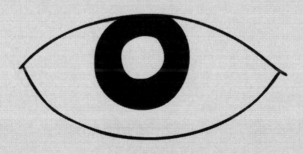

THE CREATOR

SUPERPOWERS

Inventive, possibility-focused, curious, energizing, playful, generative, game-changing, wild-at-heart, enlivening, visionary, organic, imaginative, spontaneous, meaningful, seeking-interpretations, hopeful, enthusiastic, funny, optimistic, artistic

ADDICTIONS

Entitled, escapist, fantasizing, delusional, day-dreamy, airy, tricksy, hard-to-pin-down, superficial, addicted-to-beauty/newness, impractical, foolish, idealistic

ALLERGIES

Passive, bored, static, stuck, despondent, empty, impotent, apathetic, nihilistic, unimaginative, uninspired, conforming, gloomy, dispirited, uniform, dull, lifeless

THE CONNECTOR

SUPERPOWERS

Trustworthy, generous, appreciative, compassionate, present, seeking-belonging, harmonious, intuitive, collaborative, forgiving, caring, interconnected, interdependent, kind, gentle, receptive, attentive, sensitive, open-hearted, reciprocal

ADDICTIONS

Melodramatic, sentimental, moody, gossipy, enmeshed, hypersensitive, needy, co-dependent, people-pleasing, fawning, addicted-to-consensus/conciliation

ALLERGIES

Aloof, 'cool,' blunt, frosty, fragmented, isolated, antisocial, abrupt, being-an-outsider, guarded, hidden away, numb, neglectful, avoidant, withdrawn, detached, distant, cold

Printed in Great Britain
by Amazon

16711613R00075